The Cou with the Spirit to Live

And If I Wake Up Tomorrow, I'm Gonna Be Pissed!

By
Glenora Wells-Sanders

Strategic Book Publishing and Rights Co.

Copyright © 2016 Glenora Wells-Sanders. All rights reserved.

No part of this book may be reproduced or transmitted in any form or by any means, graphic, electronic, or mechanical, including photocopying, recording, taping, or by any information storage retrieval system, without the permission, in writing, of the publisher. For more information, send an email to support@sbpra.net, Attention: Subsidiary Rights.

Strategic Book Publishing and Rights Co., LLC
USA | Singapore
www.sbpra.com

For information about special discounts for bulk purchases, please contact Strategic Book Publishing and Rights Co., LLC, Special Sales, at bookorder@sbpra.net.

ISBN: 978-1-68181-790-3

Dedication

This book is dedicated to everyone
whose life has been touched in some way
by CANCER.

Author's Note

Do you have cancer? Do you remember how you felt when you were first told? Or were you the mother, father, brother, sister, spouse, or best friend of someone and with them when they were told of the diagnosis? Were you told through a phone call, sitting in front of your physician, or being told of the devastating news in a family meeting?

In June of 2011, my late husband, Craig Sanders, was diagnosed with Non-Small Cell Squamous Lung Cancer.

The terminology of lung cancer was not unknown to me, but non-small cell squamous lung cancer was. But no matter how much you think you know, "until someone looks at you, until that finger points at you, you can never know how being told something like this feels." I very often remember Craig's words. I knew...had always known...that his smoking could have a negative impact on him later in life. And yes, I had encouraged him more often than not to stop. He was only fifty-three years of age. I knew many smokers who were well into their later years in life and were never affected by their smoking habits. It was not until later that I learned that his smoking was not the factor that attributed to his lung cancer. This provided little comfort, however, because he had already passed away. So like many of us who has lost someone to a cancer of any type, the question asked is always: why them? Why now? Those questions haunted me as well. We had our futures planned; we were to spend our retirement days in the retirement home we'd bought in West Virginia. But this is not a book about unanswered questions or remorse about why this had to happen to Craig. It is a book about one man's journey after his acceptance of this diagnosis. It speaks of his courage to continue to live his life each day to the fullest. It is a book about those who lived this journey with him; those whose lives were touched in some small or significant way. The news of his cancer involved phone calls to those that he thought needed to know. It also presents the caring of friends and family while visiting him in the hospital or our home in West Virginia, or allowing him to stay with them in Baltimore as he was traveling back and forth to Johns Hopkins' and the Cancer Treatment Center in Philadelphia for his treatments.

When our time in the present day ends, I think most of us want to leave some sort of legacy; we want to be remembered in some large or small way through our family ties, our work commitment, or by just having had a positive impact on someone during our journey. This book is the keeping of a promise made to Craig when he knew he was transitioning to his next phase of life. He wanted to be remembered in whatever way we as his family, friends, and acquaintances chose. He was so appreciative of those that took the special time to visit and telephone him in his final days. How was it that he gave *us* strength through those conversations and visits with him? How was it that he helped *us* make *his* transition much less painful? How could it be that he could still laugh, fish, fly an airplane, and travel when the physician stated, "There is nothing more we can do, so go and live out the rest of your life."

This book is an account of many of the personal conversations shared with me by some of our family and friends when they were called upon to be a part of this endeavor. I toiled with the idea of the title of the book with Craig before he passed; we chuckled about calling the book *Thirty Days, and I Ain't Counting*. This was because he was told by the medical team at the Cancer Treatment Center in Philadelphia that he only had about a month left once they'd determined that the cancer had metastasized to his major organs. With that news, we went on a second cruise!

In writing this book, I wanted to encompass his courage and strength, which influenced the first-half of the title. But it was my personal interview with Sherrie, one of his best friends, that provoked the second half of the title. Sherrie told me on the morning of the day after Craig had passed away, that during that night while she was helping to get him comfortable in his bed at the hospital, he whispered in her ear, "If I wake up tomorrow, I'm gonna be pissed." This statement truly pointed to his humor. Thus the title, *The Courage to Die, With the Spirit to Live (And, "If I Wake up Tomorrow, I'm Gonna Be Pissed.")* was deemed most appropriate.

Acknowledgements

There were so many who were there for Craig and me throughout one of the most challenging times of our lives. I would like to start with Pamela Pitt. When I shared with Pamela the idea of the book, she was so encouraging. When I explained to her that I did not think I could actually do the interviews personally, being that this would be too painful, she graciously asked me for the job. She worked effortlessly in interviewing the respondents via telephone conversations, emails, and even one-on-one physical interviews. Without Pam, this book would not have been completed in the timely manner that it was.

We offer special thanks to family: Drake Sanders, Craig's brother; Augustine Sanders, his stepmother, and her son Johnny; Aunt Carol Rogers; cousin Ginger Rawley; stepson Tony Wells; granddaughter Quierra Wells; God-Son and Nephew Christopher Jones; friends Sherrie Bishop, Tom Beauchamp, Dave and Jennie Spector, Robin and Michele Spector, Stan and Mary Palmer; Darlene Seay, Emanuel Brown, Happy Mitchell and Claude Dodson; Pinky Patel, employer and friend Ray Johnson, and minister Rev. Penelope Gladwell. Thank you all so much for your wonderful and candid memories shared when Pam called on you.

There were also some who were not interviewed because of their own family crises, health concerns, or just the fact that it was also too painful for them to talk about Craig. You still took the time out to come and see Craig, speak to him over the telephone, and allowed him to visit with you often. I want to humbly let you know that you were so wonderful to us and will continue to be in my prayers: family members Stephanie Sanders, sister-in-law; Jennifer Traglia-Bury, niece, and her beautiful family; Kevin, Nick (who Craig loved so much), and Little Kevin-Craig; friends Smitty and Tina, Terry Carter, Tony Ortiz, and of course Paul and Dorthea Beckham. I would also be remiss in my list of thanks if not acknowledging Dr. James K. Johnson, Craig's dentist, who took the time out to see Craig during the time when he could not get through the red tape at Hopkins for his dental needs.

During his illness and after Craig's departure, my special forces showed up: Sisters Gloria (Sissy) and Diane (Dee Dee), friends Valerie and Steve, Annie, Carol, Tina, Delores, Tony's wife Roz, and my beautiful grands, Dallas and Trinity. You made the drives to and from West Virginia to visit Craig in the hospital, you helped me prepare for the funeral services, you attended the service in West Virginia, and worked like angels for the repast, and you even stayed over to comfort and assure me that you would always be there for me, especially now that I had to live my life without Craig.

I know I will never, ever, forget you all for being there for Craig and also helping me in whatever way you were able to get through one of the most challenging and difficult times of my life. But I am also comforted by the fact that Craig was able to be there for you and make an indelible impact on your lives.

Introduction

Craig loved being listened to. He made many friends throughout the course of his life, and they lasted as his friends until the end. Some have unfortunately not been included in the book; he had that many.

Of course, there were times that he had arguments or issues with most of them.

But he was one who never held a grudge. He loved being needed, and he always felt that when he showed up in someone's life, he, she, or they would be better because of it. This would often be an issue in our marriage, because he too often internalized his friends' and family problems and issues. He took their problems to heart and had difficulty drawing the lines as to how to help. He brought their problems home. Craig was a fixer, and he felt inadequate when he could not help fix someone's problems or concerns. I never imagined that after twenty-one years of marriage, I would be writing a book about him. I always thought he would out-live me in spite of his habits of smoking and beer consumption. But after reading the conversations by his family and friends, I can now appreciate how much he meant to all of those who were a part of his life. I chose to categorize the book in five parts.

Contents

Author's Note 5
Acknowledgements 7
Introduction 9
PART I: THE DIAGNOSIS 13
PART II: CONVERSATIONS WITH FAMILY 27
Chapter 1: DRAKE SANDERS 29
Chapter 2: AUGUSTINE SANDERS 32
Chapter 3: GINGER RAWLEY 34
Chapter 4: CAROL ROGERS 39
Chapter 5: TONY WELLS 41
Chapter 6: QUIERRA WELLS 44
Chapter 7: CHRISTOPHER JONES 47
PART III: CONVERSATIONS WITH FRIENDS 51
Chapter 8: STAN AND MARY PALMER 55
Chapter 9: SHERRIE BISHOP 58
Chapter 10: TOM BEAUCHAMP 62
Chapter 11: DAVE AND JENNY SPECTOR 65
Chapter 12: ROBIN AND MICHELE SPECTOR 67
Chapter 13: RAY JOHNSON 71
Chapter 14: PINKY PATEL 74
Chapter 15: DARLENE SEAY 77
Chapter 16: HAPPY MITCHELL AND CLAUDE DODSON 80
Chapter 17: EMANUEL BROWN 84
Chapter 18: REVEREND PENELOPE GLADWELL 87
Chapter 19: OTHER FRIENDS 90
Chapter 20: THE FINAL THIRTY DAYS 93
Chapter 21: PAMELA PITT'S TRIBUTE 100

PART I:

THE DIAGNOSIS

"You better go and see about that cough," I remember saying to Craig. "And if you are going to stay home today, then make an appointment with the doctor." After a moment I added, "You may have a touch of pneumonia." I thought to myself that it must be pneumonia, bronchitis or even a cold that he couldn't shake, at the least.

Craig had been coughing for about two weeks or so. This was in April of 2011. You see, Craig was a smoker, and it was common knowledge that cigarette smoking was hazardous to one's health. And, given that a persistent cough for a cigarette smoker could be one of the early symptoms of lung disease was of grave concern to me.

Reluctantly, Craig took my advice and made an appointment to see his primary care physician the following week. The cough subsided to some degree; however, his PCP (Primary Care Physician) suggested after listening to his lungs that he should still have a chest X-ray. He was well aware of Craig's smoking history and had also encouraged him to quit. Craig did make some efforts to quit a couple of times, but he really enjoyed smoking and did not wish to give it up. He'd had an X-ray of his lungs about two years earlier and there were no concerns at that time.

When the call came from his physician about a week later we

both got a little concerned. Craig called me at work and told me that "something did not look good" on the X-ray. The report from the X-ray performed revealed an abnormality in his left lung and more diagnostic testing would need to take place. I remember having a sick feeling in my stomach after that conversation. I tried reassuring Craig that this could mean anything, or nothing, and after hanging up from him, I closed the door to my office and prayed.

Craig always picked me up from work in his work van when I chose not to drive. By then we had sold our home in Maryland and were down to our countdown before at least my retirement. We had been driving to and from our home in West Virginia for about three years with little difficulty. He loved the drive to and from. This was our quality time, except for the times he was calling the state troopers on drivers that he chose to report for whatever he thought was inappropriate in their driving: speeding, changing lanes without signaling, driving the emergency lane when there were back-ups, etc. I could never understand why he felt as though he needed to be the highway patrol officer. The fact that he drove home every day hiding his beer in his lap and drinking it on the drive home was inconsequential to him. But this particular evening the drive home was different. Craig did not seem to care about what any of the other drivers were doing. The hour-and-a-half drive was quiet and contemplative by us both. The next day we continued with our morning routine of driving to work. I don't think either of us got much sleep that night. Craig's demeanor was very abrupt and short during the ride in. He started talking about not being ready to die. I stopped his words and became annoyed that he was thinking so negatively. I was always the positive one in any situation we encountered, so I refused to allow him to give up before anything had really been confirmed.

We met with a specialist at Johns Hopkins' Sydney Kimmel Cancer Center to discuss the next course of action after the CAT (computerized axial tomography) scan of the chest had been done. The physician discussed with us that the CAT scan had revealed, "…a 4.6 x 3.2 cm mass that appeared to be in the anterior aspect of the right lobe abutting the aorta and sternum." He also stated that Craig appeared to have a 2x1 cm station center lymph node along with a possible small 10R lymph node as well. He discussed with us plans to proceed with diagnostic sampling—a bronchoscopy—and possibly a biopsy of the tissue if the bronchoscopy was non-diagnostic. He was also asked to obtain a PET (positron emission tomography) scan for further staging work-up.

By then Craig had stopped smoking and was on a smoking cessation plan as well as medication for anxiety. The specialist was a renowned one at Hopkins. We researched him before we went to see him, so we felt that we could feel confident in the course of action he advised. The discussion seemed hopeful at the time. He asked Craig what had made him decide to go to the doctor. Craig pointed to me and stated, "She did." He quickly added, "She said if I couldn't make it to work, I better call the doctor today, so that's what I ended up doing."

"Well, that's a good thing," the specialist replied. "She may have saved your life."

I then looked at Craig, smiled with a smirk, and said, "See that, you really owe me now!"

We all laughed. The discussion then took a more serious note about the possible outcomes of the biopsy, meaning that if the mass was cancerous, what the course of action would be. Having worked in the field of healthcare, I felt I could ask intelligent questions. Craig too had been on a roller coaster ride with the loss of his mother first and then his father; he was well-versed in options available for many major diseases and illnesses. But, we were not there yet, so the specialist advised us to wait until we knew for sure. The appointment was then made to have the diagnostic testing done. I later learned that I was not the only person getting on Craig to see his doctor. Ray, his friend and employer, had also encouraged him. I know we both wished at the time we were encouraging him to go and get that cough checked out that it would have resulted in a better outcome, but it did not.

After leaving Johns Hopkins that evening, our drive home seemed a little more upbeat. In retrospect, I am glad that we made that move to have West Virginia be our permanent residence. Craig must have glimpsed into his future. I remember him once saying, "Why wait another five or six years before retiring permanently when we need to enjoy our home now?" We decided that certainly, some sacrifices would be made as far as getting up in the morning and coming home later in the evenings, but he felt that we were able to make the transition and we did. He used to also say to me, "Knowing you, Cookie, you like being too busy, you ain't never really totally retiring anyway." In addition, at that time, we were going through an economic downturn in the mortgage industry, which resulted in us, like so many others, owing more on our home than it was worth, making us 'upside down' in our mortgage in Maryland. So this was an advisable move financially. Every time we pulled up to our home in West Virginia, Craig would smile. Often times on the weekends, he would pull open the vertical blinds and look out at the lake with his can of beer in his hand and remark, "This is effing ridiculous."

I was at work the day Craig called me. I could tell from the sound of his voice that the news was not good. Craig rarely called me by my actual name; we always had various nicknames for each other throughout the course of our marriage. But that particular morning he called me Cookie. I knew then that the words following would be dreaded for the rest of my life.

"Cookie," he said, "I just got off the phone with the doctor. I have lung cancer, and he wants me to come in."

My head began to spin, I was dizzy and told Craig, "Hold on for a second." I could barely muster the strength to close and lock my office door. When I got back on the phone, the tears then began to roll down my face. I had no words to say at the time; I could only sigh and cry silently. I am not certain where the rest of my staff or colleagues were at that exact time. Generally, in the course of my work day, someone is always knocking on my door, ringing my phone, or paging me overhead. It seemed at that time, that the forces in the universe were operating in my favor to give me a few moments of uninterrupted time so I could just cry quietly with my husband as he was given the most tragic news of his life.

I then heard Craig say, "Cookie, it's going to be okay."

I replied, "Yes, we will get through this."

Craig then said, "The doc wants me to come and see him today. Are you available today?"

I asked, "What time?" He told me within the hour. I replied, "Do you want me to come and get you?"

Craig insisted, "No, I will call you when I'm outside."

I told him that I would be outside in my car waiting for him. I needed to be alone to digest the news. I emailed my manager and told her that I had to leave for a while regarding an urgent matter pertaining to my husband's health. I then went to my car and waited for Craig to have me go with him so that we could hear the news together again.

That was the beginning of a journey that I never wanted to experience. The news of stage 3-A lung cancer was devastating to us. The PET-CAT scan indicated that a mass was in the upper right lobe of his lung with possible invasion of the chest wall and mediastinum. Craig seemed to lose color in his face when his physician stated it was that advanced. He knew that people with lung cancer could have surgery to remove the tumor, even if that meant living with only one lung. He thought surgery would be a viable option in his case. His physician did not seem optimistic about surgery in his case; however, he was not the expert in this field. He then scheduled Craig to see another specialist to speak about the treatment options, and we did.

We so wanted the surgery, but the location of the mass made surgery not advisable. It was located very close to the aorta. After meeting with the specialist at Johns Hopkins, we learned that the disease was only in that area of his lung, and we felt blessed that the PET scan showed no invasion to the brain or any other area of his body at that time. The best course of action would be chemotherapy and then radiation. For the next five or six months, Craig started a course of chemotherapy and radiation at Johns Hopkins. His adventurous spirit then began to emerge.

After a few weeks of treatment, he would meet with the radiologist and oncologist to get an update as to whether the cancer had continued to advance or slow up. He would also have to get the PET scans over those times for more conclusive evidence. We saw quite a few people in this medical arena during that time and I will say that I do believe that some can be much more compassionate and caring than others. In essence, some have been doing their jobs too long, and it exudes in their bedside manner.

I will never forget our first Thanksgiving during that time. About a month or two before the holiday, he was told that the larger mass had diminished in size. There were a couple of other tumors that had been shown on the PET scan that were also being treated. This was such good news. We really got our hopes up! During that summer and into late fall, we began to resume most of our activities. Craig even attempted to go back to work. He never got sick from the chemotherapy either. His energy level had slowed, but his spirit was good overall. At that time, there was discussion of the benefits of marijuana for the nausea that so often accompanies chemotherapy. He asked his physicians if he had the opportunity to obtain any would there be a problem with him still receiving his treatment. He was not advised either way.

Life has a way at times of throwing you more than one curve ball at a time. During that time, we were given bad news regarding my health. A very small malignant lump was found in my left breast which resulted in me opting for surgery and chemotherapy. Still, we could not be deterred. Why would we? Craig had many tales of narrow escapes during his life and he was still here. Cancer was just another inconvenience; he could beat it. I had also had my share of narrow escapes during my lifetime, (not as many as Craig's though), so a little lump was inconsequential to me. I had "God's Favor."

We were a great match and source of strength for each other. Unfortunately, during the week of Thanksgiving, his oncologist called him following another PET scan. Craig was asked to come in for another consultation. She reported that the cancer was growing again and was beginning to occupy more of his lung capacity. She wanted him to consider participating in a trial drug therapy study to test a new drug. The trial treatments offered no guarantees for prolonging his life. He wouldn't even know whether he was being given the new drug or a placebo.

Craig became furious, feeling that his oncologist seemed to be giving up on him. She offered nothing else, except to see him as some experimental guinea pig (or so we thought). Craig let his oncologist know in no uncertain terms how he felt about being asked to participate in this program. What a way to celebrate Thanksgiving! The dinner was over at my sister's house. Craig remained upstairs in her bedroom at that time and had no appetite for the meal. He always loved to eat. That was a sure sign that he had become very discouraged.

When I told my son Tony how bleak things were looking, he advised me to give the Cancer Treatment Centers of America a call. I can remember it being the Sunday afternoon after Thanksgiving. We were home in West Virginia. I was a little hesitant in making the call because I wasn't sure how receptive Craig would be after the discouraging news from his oncologist at Johns Hopkins during the week of Thanksgiving.

I called and spoke to the person who answered about Craig. She was very reassuring and understanding. She suggested I have Craig give her a call so that she could learn more about his situation. I prayed and then spoke to Craig about the Cancer Treatment Center. Surprisingly enough, he was receptive to speaking to the representative. We were even blessed that they would accept our insurance. So another adventure began, to and from the Cancer Treatment Center in Philadelphia, Pennsylvania.

We began to live our lives again, and that January of 2012, we decided to take a cruise from Baltimore to Florida and then Bermuda. I had stopped traveling with Craig for a while, too embarrassing at times, as he was always complaining about one thing or the other. But we had a new lease on life, for us both, and I didn't want to share that with anyone else. The whole time we were on the cruise, Craig had no problem telling every and anyone about his cancer diagnosis. He was to have stopped drinking and smoking. But on the cruise, he stopped neither. It was fine with me; I wanted him to really enjoy himself and he did. He would come to the cabin sometimes late at night after I had already turned in, singing to the top of his lungs. Singing and dancing were not his strong suits. He had only "white-boy moves." He made several "friends" on the cruise who told me how brave they thought he was, and how much of an impact he made on them in the short time they had interacted with him. I'm sure he will always remain in their minds.

I don't think I will ever again experience anything like what the Cancer Treatment Center in Philadelphia provided to us in my life when it comes to an illness, and if Craig were here, he would say the same. Arrangements were made by the travel team at the Treatment Center for our train rides to and from Philadelphia, along with accommodations for staying over for treatments at two great hotels. Our transportation was arranged with Amtrak. The first time we arrived at the train station, we were met by a tall African-American gentleman who had a flyer with our names on it to indicate that he would be our driver to the Center. We acknowledged that we were the Sanders, and he put his arms around us first and then began to pray on our behalf. Craig was not much of a praying man; I was the church-goer in the family. When Craig's father used to call him on Sunday mornings to see what he was up to, he would ask Craig, "You go to church today, boy?" Craig would often reply, "No, but I sent my representative." This became a standing joke of ours. Craig was raised Catholic, but when he and I married, he joined my church: Mt. Ararat Baptist. I had hoped we would be going to church more often. The few times he went with me he fell asleep. He was so turned off by the ministers asking for "soft" money during offering times. I got to the place where I would never let him know what I was giving for my tithes. He would be turning over in his grave if he were in one! But, I do believe that as time continued on in his illness, he developed a true personal relationship with God.

When Craig looked up at this tall African-American gentleman praying with us in the train station, a smile came on his face; I then knew we were off to a good start. The next day we were met by the clinical team. Each member of the team, from the oncologist to the radiologist, to the clinical nutritionist and so forth, met with us to go over the current diagnosis and what we hoped would be a positive outcome. We never had to leave the discussion room. They all came to us one by one. A treatment plan was put in place by the clinical team, and from February of 2012 through late July, we traveled back and forth to Philadelphia.

We ate like never before. The Center had a restaurant on the premises that offered meals prepared by great chefs. The variety of the food was unheard of. Craig and I enjoyed those times in our hotel room and during our meals. He even insisted on getting his prescription for Viagra filled. The chemo had some serious side effects, however. There were times when he spiked a fever and would have to stay a day or more over what we had anticipated. He never was pleased about this. One of the chemo therapies resulted in him having serious hives. Another time, thrush filled his mouth and his tongue became badly inflamed. None of the wonderful meals could be tolerated at the restaurant because eating was not enjoyable.

I left work on several occasions and took the train up to stay over when his temperatures would spike and he could not return home the same day. Craig was self-employed, so I continued to work as long as he felt strong enough to ride into town to stay with his friend Smitty in between his treatments in Philadelphia. I had opted to receive radiation for myself to err on the side of safety, and that way Craig did not have to feel so alone. I arranged my days with his days so that we could ride to and from together. I wanted to be with him any way I could.

There were even times that once we got back home in West Virginia, he would spike a temperature and we would have to go to City Hospital in town. The nurses were wonderful; however, Craig had no kinds words about the doctors there. Once during a stay there from a high temperature, he insisted on being transferred back to the Cancer Treatment Center in Philadelphia, and he was. He felt that the hospital team there was very inadequate. I can remember climbing in those small hospital beds that looked like something from the 1950s. The rooms were so cold looking and bleak. Craig would sweat through his gown and even the sheets during some of those hospital stays. The nurses would come in and give us both a change of gowns and change the sheets as he would soak them so badly from his perspiration. His oncologist referred to this as "tumor fever."

Craig was often termed the "customer from hell" during his home-improvement career. During his illness, I termed him the "patient from hell." He was very adept about what should be happening to him regarding treatments, and very knowledgeable overall regarding his medications and the administration of them. There was no fooling him about any of that. I couldn't even imagine that he would have any issues with the team at the Cancer Treatment Center, but he did. His concerns went all the way up to Administration and were quickly addressed.

Craig really believed in his oncologist at Cancer Treatment Center. He never had an unkind word to say about her. When the PET scan revealed that a more aggressive form of treatment should be administered because the current chemo was not slowing down the growth of the tumors, she advised him of another chemo treatment plan and Craig agreed. Month after month, we took the trip to Philadelphia. Craig's appetite had begun to decline. He was fearful of having to receive a feeding tube, so a plan for increasing his appetite was put in place. By then, he began to have more discomfort in his breathing. He met with another radiologist at the Center who suggested that he receive another round of radiation to shrink the tumor so that he would not be as uncomfortable in his breathing. In this round of treatment, his chest became so darkened; he looked as though he had been in the sun for weeks. He hardly complained though, he was so drugged up during that time.

I became so concerned with the drugs that he was taking; he was on so many. I worried that he would overdose on his meds so I began to administer them to him or I would leave them out to take so I could keep an accurate account of what and how much he was taking. He was told that pain should not be an issue. Unfortunately, by the beginning of July, any chance of this cancer going into remission was discouraging. I left work that day with plans to stay with Craig that weekend. By then, I was finished with my treatment and doing well. I had completed my FMLA forms and knew that the time had now come to leave work and concentrate totally on Craig.

I had planned a cruise for us the end of July of 2012 with my granddaughter Quierra, my close friend Pinky, and her children Reena and Amar. Craig wasn't interested in going on this one. He was comfortable with the fact that his friend Sherrie and her family would be keeping him company in West Virginia during my trip. He also felt that I needed a break.

I arrived in Philadelphia that evening by Amtrak as usual and was met by the limo driver as many times before. Sometimes we got the same limo drivers as we made our way to and from the train station, most of the time they were different. However, they were always pleasant and accommodating. Sometimes there would be other cancer patients in the limo with me; other times I would be alone. I would say to myself that this was just one treatment center of many. How could there be so many others around the country? *Why is there so much cancer*, I wondered, as I looked around at so many different faces in the limo and inside the facility.

I remember going to Craig's room and feeling like something was dreadfully wrong. I walked into his room and gave him a kiss as I would normally do. Craig was never a large man, and he had never weighed over a hundred and twenty-eight pounds soaking wet. He was now down to about a hundred pounds. At home, I would fix protein shakes to keep his weight over a hundred pounds. We would get excited when a weight gain of three or more pounds took place. That day Craig then took me by my hands. These words will never, ever leave my mind: "I don't have much time," he said.

I froze, and no words would come out. He went on to say that the cancer was in his major organs and the oncologist would be coming up to talk to me in a little while about going home for good. I then sobbed in Craig's arms, and I cried, "No, no, this can't be, no, no, you can't leave me."

Craig was so comforting to me as I continued to cry in his arms. He seemed to have already come to terms with his fate. He then said to me, "Cookie, stop, you know I will never leave you."

Right at that time, one of the medical doctors came in to discuss the recent prognosis. I believe she was his guardian angel that showed up right in time before the oncologist came in. She said that it was time for Craig to "go and live out the rest of his life."

When she said that, I asked about how much more time he had. She said it could be a month, a couple of weeks, but that only God knew for sure. I then asked could he go on a cruise. She replied, "Of course, if that's what he wants."

I looked at Craig and said, "Come on, honey, it will take your mind off of things." I also asked her if she could get him a prescription to start him on his prednisone again as that was the only drug that would make him eat. She agreed to getting him on the prednisone and he agreed to going on the cruise. By then, the oncologist walked in and our plan of action was discussed with her. She did not seem to think our new plans—the cruise or the prednisone—were in the best interests of Craig; however, she conceded and we planned to leave the next day to finish the rest of our lives together.

The rest of that night at the hospital at the Cancer Treatment Center was so very sad. Craig and I began to call our family and friends to let them know that the medical team there had no other treatments for him. He was just given a few weeks or less to live. We were both crying to our family and friends as we told them of the news. Not everyone was called that night. I can remember distinctly calling my sisters, my son, my granddaughter, and a few of my closest friends. I can remember Pinky wanting to drive up to Philadelphia to drive me back home. If one ever drove with Pinky, one would understand how emphatic I was that she not drive up to Philadelphia to take me back to Baltimore. Besides, Craig needed me in one piece! I am not sure who Craig called, but I'm sure the first person had to be his brother Drake and the second person had to be Stan.

Once we made it back to West Virginia, pretty much all of our friends and family were called. Craig and I made the cruise by the end of July as planned. When we got back, family and friends then began to call and visit. Craig lived past the thirty days he was told. His last couple of months were filled with visits and phone calls and great times. Here are some of these conversations shared by those family members and friends during those last days.

PART II:

CONVERSATIONS WITH FAMILY

Chapter 1
DRAKE SANDERS

Drake was Craig's one and only older brother. While they had similar interests, I think of Drake as being completely the opposite of Craig. He was always composed, reserved, and practical in all of his endeavors. His tone of voice was always calming and subdued. I don't ever remember a time when I heard him yell or scream at anyone. Drake was also Craig's best friend. But Craig had several best friends, although Drake was chosen to be the best man at our wedding.

Throughout our marriage, Craig would visit Drake and his wife Steph at their home in Baltimore. When I would accompany Craig on his visits, I knew that I had to prepare for a long visit. The two of them would get together and have their own private conversations that would sometimes last for hours and could only be deciphered by them. Steph and I knew we had to take a back seat to the two of them whenever there would be a visit. Often times Craig would visit Drake without me. That way he didn't have to look at my face of annoyance wanting to get home after a while.

I used to ask him, "What in the world could you two be talking about so much? You just saw Drake last week!" But it never mattered to Craig, as he loved seeing and talking to his big brother.

During our marriage, Craig lost both of his parents. He lost his mother first, and then his father, both unexpectedly. His parents were divorced when he and I met; however, he still kept an amicable and wonderful relationship with them both, in spite of how hurt he was during that time. His mother's illness was one that I will never forget.

Drake and Craig did a phenomenal job taking care of their mom. Their mom, Marie, who I would often refer to as Flossie May, was one whose personality was very infectious. She loved life and I could see so much of her personality reflected in Craig. When she became terminally ill, Craig would leave work and drive to Drake's house to continue to help his brother take care of Marie. By then, she had been totally moved out of her home and resided with Drake and his wife Steph. This was *such* a trying time in our marriages. Craig would be getting home very late at night, only to start all over the next day to repeat the same routine. The idea of having to place their mom in a nursing home to live out the rest of her days was unconscionable to both brothers. Drake and Craig were the only two left of the Sanders' legacy. Neither had children of their own; however, they were both wonderful parents to Steph's two, and my one, from previous marriages.

After his call to me, Drake was the first person Craig called when he got the news about his cancer diagnosis. We were at Johns Hopkins. The previous X-ray showed suspicion about the mass in his lung, but the biopsy confirmed that he indeed had lung cancer, but the course of treatment was not certain until we met with the specialist. Craig called Drake before he even left the hospital to let him know that surgery was not an option. I could hear his voice quiver as he spoke to his one and only brother. The tears then began to roll down Craig's face. Drake was a huge part of the year and a half of this new journey with his brother. It looked pretty positive at first, but as time continued on, we all realized the cancer was going to have its way. This is what Drake had to say to the Interviewer…

Q: What would you say about the title of the book regarding Craig?

A: I like the title of the book. Especially the "If I Wake-Up Tomorrow, I'm Gonna Be Pissed" part.

Q: Can you remember the first conservation you had with Craig about his diagnosis?

A: I remember the call I received from Craig. I could immediately tell by the sound of his voice that something was seriously wrong. He told me he had cancer and that it was bad. He was so scared…for himself, but more for everyone else that he knew and loved. His big concern was for the well-being of those he would be leaving behind.

Q: What was your response and reaction to the news?

A: I felt the blood draining from my head, and thought I was going to faint. I was afraid for him...what treatments he would have to endure, what the long-term prognosis would be after treatment. I was afraid for myself...how I would get by without my brother. There wasn't much I could say, nothing I could do but to share a cry with him. I wished I could tell him that everything would be fine.

Q: How often did you meet with him during this time?

A: I met with him several times. He would sometimes visit after he had a treatment. He almost always had an upbeat positive attitude. When he started losing his hair, he came over to my house and we had a head-shaving party. He made it fun, trying out different hairstyles, from Mohawk to fully bald. On days when the therapy made him sick and weak he would sit quietly, without complaint, during the visit.

Q: How was your life changed or impacted while visiting and talking with him in his final days?

A: Craig taught me what real courage looks like. He set an example for me on how to enjoy the life we have, and how to let go of that life with grace.

Q: What is your fondest memory of Craig?

A: Craig and I have shared so much. It's hard to pick just one. I loved his ability to make friends everywhere he went. I'll never forget his weekend visits to my dorm when I was in college. Him encouraging me to take the ski lift to the top of the hill, and getting me to go scuba diving. His devotion and dedication to help care for our mother when she was ill. I remember our daily drives to Washington, D.C. to see our father when he was hospitalized with a fatal condition.

Q: If you could share or say anything to him today, what would that be?

A: I would tell him that I loved him, not just as a brother, but also as the dear lifelong friend that he was. I cherish the time we shared together. I would thank him for making his final departure one filled with peace. His gracious acceptance of death gave me comfort.

Chapter 2
AUGUSTINE SANDERS

Augustine, Craig's stepmother, married Craig's father; 'Dad' as I called him in his later years. Craig was very happy for his father when he and Augustine married. He wanted his dad to have a partner to share his later years with. He would often refer to her as his step-mom. Craig and I often had our annual Father's Day cookouts for several years before the passing of both of our dads; Augustine always joined us for those occasions. Craig and Augustine had a special relationship. He seemed to know that it meant a lot to his dad to have her indoctrinated into our families. This was so easy for him because he loved helping people be happy. When Dad became ill, Craig often communicated with Augustine late at night, always trying to reassure her that he would be okay.

Both Dad and Augustine were raised Catholic and they took their religion seriously. I never saw so many people of that faith in such merriment as I did at their wedding. When Craig's dad passed away, he continued to remain in touch with Augustine. The news of his diagnosis affected Augustine deeply. This is what Augustine had to say...

Q: What do you think about the title of the book?

A: I really liked the first part of the title—The Courage to Die with the Spirit to Live. But I don't like the second part of the title. I wouldn't use it if I were writing the book.

Q: Can you remember the first conversation you had with Craig about his cancer diagnosis?

A: Craig was always upbeat and he thought he would beat the diagnosis. He was more concerned about Cookie's health and breast cancer diagnosis at the same time. I really thought he would beat it too. Ernest (Craig's father) and I were concerned about his smoking so much but because he was being treated at Hopkins and then later, the Cancer Treatment Center of Philadelphia...with him being so young and all the latest and modern technology that they have today, I thought he would beat the cancer. But when the Cancer Treatment Center told him there was nothing else they could do, I was surprised and sad.

Q: How much time were you able to spend with him during his final days?

A: I did not get to spend too much time with Craig because he lived in West Virginia and I live outside D.C., but we did get to talk three or four times a week on the phone and we always ended our calls with "I love you." As sick as Craig was, he always mustered enough strength and energy to talk and make you laugh. He even told my son Johnnie how to make a drink using ginger beer, with a particular kind of ginger beer, dark rum, and lime juice, that he (Johnnie) still drinks and enjoys to this day. He even asked me to cook him some chitterlings one day and I don't cook them because they stink. And I learned later on that Drake had stopped at Lexington Market one day and took them to him.

Q: What are your fondest memories of Craig?

A: My fondest memory of Craig is that he was the "king" of barbecue. They always had a Father's Day celebration every year at their house on Annellen Road. But after Cookie's father died, they didn't have them anymore. The last cookout was at Drake's house and Craig did all the cooking. He loved to barbecue.

Q: If there was one thing you could say to Craig today, what would you say?

A: If I could say anything to him today, it would be that I am still enjoying the lovely bathroom that he did for me. It is beautiful and I would say "thank you." I would tell him to stop smoking those awful cigarettes, and most of all, I would let him know that I love him very much. It's making me tear up right now just talking about him. Craig will always hold a special place in my heart.

Chapter 3
GINGER RAWLEY

Craig was so happy when his mother and his cousin Ginger became reacquainted in his adult life. He was in awe of how successful she and her husband Vaughn had become. It meant a lot to him to "brag" on his cousin and her beautiful family.

I always remember Ginger as being so kind and approachable. When there was an opportunity for any family celebrations, Ginger and Vaughn were always there. I can still remember them being at our wedding, and the celebration of Craig's 40th birthday. I never saw Ginger's husband Vaughn laugh or even crack a smile until Craig was in of front of him talking about who knows what. When Craig learned that they had a tax consultant business, he was adamant about the fact that we would be having them do our taxes for as long as they remained in business.

I am not certain as to when Craig telephoned Ginger. I just knew that she had to be in one of the "top five" on the list. And as expected, even with her own family circumstances that kept her busy, she was there for him. Ginger and Vaughn offered us a place in their beautiful home during the time Craig had to go back and forth to receive his chemotherapy treatments. Ginger even volunteered to take Craig to his scheduled treatments for as long as he needed her. Craig was so appreciative of her adjusting her schedule so that he would not have to be a burden on me or anyone else. This was the early part of our journey with the diagnosis.

Here is what Ginger had to say…

Q: What would you say about the title of the book regarding Craig?

A: Although my cousin Craig came into my life when we were both adults, we had an instant connection that was heart-warming as well as hilarious. He was a person to whom life was very special. I believe that the title of the book suits him well. I had never met anyone who lived life to the fullest each and every day. He had the ability to make you see the importance of *life* and the unimportance of *things*. His spirit was evident in the way he treated his friends and family. Once he understood that he was not going to get better and would not be able to live on his own terms, I believe he would definitely have been completely pissed off if he had to awaken to that sentence one more day. I can't think of anyone who made me laugh harder (with the exception of his mother and my sister). He was small in stature but had a giant spirit that made me think he could do anything.

Q: Do you remember your first conversations about Craig after learning of his diagnosis?

A: My husband and I were in Detroit at the Henry Ford Museum when my cell phone rang and I saw that it was Craig calling. We didn't talk that often, but whenever we did, the conversations were always happy and filled with silly talk. Most often with Craig making fun of my husband, who is a very serious-minded guy. I remember saying, "Hey, where have you been?" He immediately told me that he'd been diagnosed with lung cancer. I was so stunned that my mind could not process what he'd said. I had to sit down on a bench, and my husband kept asking me, "What's wrong?" He thought someone had died. Craig said my name [Ginger], and I was finally able to say, "What?" He repeated the diagnosis. I told Craig that we would be home in one or two days and that we should talk about what the next steps would be then. When I got off the phone, I told my husband that I couldn't believe what I'd heard. I started to cry right there at the Henry Ford Museum. The friends we were traveling with came over to see what had happened. I just couldn't understand what was happening. My husband tried to make me feel better by telling me how cancer treatments have come a long way and the cure rates have dramatically improved. All I could think of was how awful the treatments were when I'd gone to chemo with my husband's cousin a few years ago. It was hard to watch. The next conversation I had about Craig was with my sister. She is a very spiritual person and the best prayer person I know. If you need a prayer, call on her! She felt very sad that Craig was facing this challenge. I was still numb and not thinking clearly. I don't remember if Craig and I talked the day we returned to Maryland or a few days later. I do remember talking to him by phone and then he and Cookie coming over to our house. Craig needed someone to go to his treatments with him because Cookie was also facing her own health challenge and was undergoing treatment. I was honored that he asked me to help. I wanted him to just stay at our house but he insisted that he would drive to our house and then I could take him for treatment.

Q: What was your response and reaction to the news?

A: Again, I was shocked and wanted to help in any way I could.

Q: How often did you have the opportunity to spend time with him?

A: I went to chemo and radiation with him during the time Cookie was undergoing her treatment. I remember the treatment took the entire day. We started with chemo and then went to radiation. At that time, I didn't realize a person could have both in the same day. He laid on a bed or maybe a big chair for the chemo. I know he could feel it running into his arm and through his body. I didn't know if it hurt; it did not seem so. He never complained. He only worried about me being able to get something to eat or drink. I remember the room being full of cancer patients getting chemo. I tried to focus on Craig. We spent the time talking about our family. My grandmother and his mother's grandmother were sisters. I told him everything I knew about the Parker women. They were of strong stock and knew how to take care of their families, many of them on their own. When my family moved to Maryland, my mom kept telling me to find her cousin. I thought the odds of us finding Marie were pretty small. Anyway, my mother came to visit and somehow had tracked down a name and number for Marie (Craig's mother). I called her, not expecting a positive response. Marie, however, was overjoyed to hear from me and we all became fast friends. My mother was so happy. Her whole goal had been that Marie understand that she had family on her mother's side who loved her and had never forgotten her and her brothers.

Craig and I talked about these things, as well as how my daughter had fallen in total love with him as a six- or seven-year-old. He came to her birthday party and he might as well have been the only guest. He brought her a purse for her birthday. She may still have that purse! She was completely heartbroken when Craig and Cookie got married. She was to marry Craig herself! We laughed about that and other funny things.

After accompanying Craig to a couple of treatments, we just talked on the phone. He was very happy to be able to go on a cruise and said he'd actually gained a few pounds. He said that cruise was 'the best vacation ever'. I was elated at the news he had gained weight. He laughed when I told him that I wished there was a way to suck the fat out of my butt and squash it into him! I'm not clear on when this particular conversation occurred, but one of his doctors thought he was the most remarkable patient he had ever treated. I believe it was one of the physicians at Johns Hopkins. It was shortly afterward it seemed as though the treatments were working. I said, "Of course they're working." There could never be enough time to spend with him.

Q: How has your life changed or been impacted by visiting and talking with him in his final days?

A: Honestly, it never crossed my mind that he would die. I felt that he was going to beat this disease and return to burning the candle at both ends. In fact, when Cookie called to tell, me she must have used his phone. I looked at the caller ID and saw that it was Craig and I was happy to hear from him. I can't tell you how wonderful it was to find this part of my family. From our initial meeting, I felt as though we'd known each other all our lives. It makes me smile just to think of our relationship.

Q: What were some of your fondest memories of Craig?

A: My fondest memories involve watching how my daughter at

age six or seven was totally smitten by her cousin. She'd draw him pictures that he'd later hang in his bedroom. I remember when Craig came over to refinish the floors in our old house in Catonsville, the machine he was going to use weighed more than he did. My husband said there was no way Craig would be able to tame that monster piece of machinery, but tame it he did. The whole process was not without problems and lots of laughter. He never took himself too seriously and reminded us to do the same. Craig could drink more beer than anyone I've ever known. About six or eight of us once took a road trip to North Carolina, (It could have been South Carolina, I can't remember which) to see buggy races. We were traveling in a van and the guys were drinking beer all the way down the road. (That's not legal is it?) We finally arrived at this wonderful old hotel. It reminded us of the Antebellum South. The other guests were pretty stoic and straight-laced. Well, we rolled out of the van at the front door laughing and acting pretty silly and a beer bottle rolled out and landed at the feet of the guy helping with the bags. Needless to say, we all roared with laughter. That was the beginning of a great road trip.

Because I am a notoriously bad cook, Craig teased me endlessly about cooking. If I offered him food, he'd give me that side-eyed look and say, "Let me think about that."

Q: If there were something you could say to or share with Craig today, what would that be?

A: If I could say one more thing to my dear cousin, it would be, "Thank you for enriching my life with your love, charm, and wit. I will never forget you."

Chapter 4
CAROL ROGERS

"Aunt Carol" was how Craig referred to her. They were somehow related through Craig's dad Ernest. I am not certain as to whether Carol was his cousin or his aunt. I just knew she was very pivotal in keeping the Duvall and Sanders legacy going. Carol was one of those persons in the family who was relied upon to keep everyone else informed of the other family members' important information, be it the marriages, births, deaths, attained accomplishments, and so forth. She was instrumental in the news noted in the family newspaper that was written and available to all of us monthly. It allowed me to know and interact with Craig's family on any occasion. One of the all-time favorites was the annual crab feast. True, it was a collaborative effort on the part of all of the Duvalls and Sanders; however, I would not be far from inaccurate in stating that Carol was the "glue" for this wonderful annual event.

As life would have it, Carol became very involved in seeing to the care of her immediate family members, so she was not able to be as active in the kinds of activities that I remember when Craig and I first married. Seems a shame that today there has been no one to follow in Carol's shoes for such wonderful events. Perhaps one day maybe someone will be willing to take the baton and run with it like Carol.

When Craig became ill, Carol was also another person he chose to share his illness with. Here are Carol's responses to the interviewer's questions...

Q: What would you say about the title of the book regarding Craig?

A: I love the title; sounds like something Craig would say.

Q: Do you remember your first conversations about Craig after learning of his diagnosis?

A: I called to see how he was doing and told him I wanted to visit. He was still optimistic and wanted visitors.

Q: What was your response and reaction to the news?

A: It's always heartbreaking when you hear about anyone having a fatal illness, especially someone young. And, because we had not seen one another in quite some time, I was completely surprised that he was ill. It hurt!

Q: How often did you have the opportunity to spend time with him?

A: I only saw Craig once during his illness and I drove my uncle and cousin to see him in West Virginia. I only spoke to him once or twice after that. The last time he was in the hospital and he was trying to explain what was going on, there was some confusion and I ended up talking with Cookie.

Q: How has your life changed or been impacted while visiting and talking with him in his final days?

A: Over the years, I have met and spoken to several friends and family members who were dealing with the finality of their life. I'm actually going through it with two friends now. Like with Craig, there's this feeling of contentment, if that's the right word. Craig seemed to make peace with himself.

Q: What are some of your fondest memories of Craig?

A: I will always remember visiting Drake and Craig at their parent's home. Craig was in a high chair and looking so much like his father. He was the devilish one. I thought he was so funny, and he was just a toddler. I always thought of him as a carefree individual.

Q: If there were something you could say or share with Craig today, what would that be?

A: I hope your transition was peaceful and I hope you felt fulfilled in your life. You were truly loved.

Chapter 5
TONY WELLS

Tony, Craig's stepson and my son, was away in the military during my dating days with Craig. I chuckle when I think of having to report to my son about who I was involved with during his time away. As is so often stated, there is no love like a love between a mother and her son. So Craig knew he had to take a backseat role to Tony. Tony's relationship with his own dad was very strained at the least. He just was not as present as he could have been. While Craig came into Tony's life when he was an adult, he made himself available as often as he could. He would refer to Tony as his son.

While away in the service, Tony's daughter, Quierra, was born. Craig embraced Quierra as his granddaughter, which was a very good starting point with Tony when he was finally discharged from the service. We allowed Tony to get stabilized in our home in Baltimore. Craig's home-improvement skills were put to great use in constructing a studio apartment for Tony on his return.

On the day of our marriage, my dad and Tony escorted me down the aisle. Craig had no opposition to having them both escort me; I was adamant about having my son escort me as well. When I spoke to Tony about having a skillset like Craig's, he embraced the idea and was hired by Craig in his business. Surprisingly enough, Tony stayed employed by Craig for a good number of years. I said surprisingly because Craig was a very meticulous and unbearable "task-master." I used to hear all of his tales at the end of the day as to how this person did not do this, or how another person did not do that, inclusive of my son. And this did not set very well with me. That would lead us into some big arguments, oftentimes with me not speaking to him for a week at a time.

Tony was not deterred for the most part. He admired Craig's knowledge and skills. What got under his craw the most was Craig actually talking about his mom (me) to him. "How does one have the nerve to do that?" Well, with Craig, it never mattered; if you made him angry about anything, you would be talked about, in no uncertain terms. He had no loyalties.

Craig would be very happy to know that his knowledge and skills taught in the home improvement/construction field still live on today by those with whom he shared his skills. When he passed away, I called on Tony to do some of the projects at home that Craig would be doing if he were still alive. I am proud of how much he learned being not only his stepson, but his employee today. This is what Tony had to say about his stepdad…

Q: What would you say about the proposed title of the book regarding Craig?

A: That definitely sounds like something Craig would say.

Q Do you remember your first conversations about Craig after learning of his diagnosis?

A: I do not remember the first conversation I had with him about his cancer diagnosis, it was something you really didn't talk to me much about.

Q: What was your response and reaction to the news?

A: I felt very, very sad; but I also felt like if anyone could beat it or figure out a way to beat it, Craig would be the one who could beat cancer.

Q: How often did you have the opportunity to spend time with him?

A: I did not spend much time with him while he was going back and forth to his treatments. But, I worked with him every day for about seven years. And, I can tell you, it was not always easy!

Q: How has your life changed or been impacted by Craig?

A: He was very supportive to me during the time I was going through a custody battle for my kids. He helped to drive my mom and the kids' grandmother to and from Georgia for the custody hearings.

Q: What are some of your fondest memories of Craig?

A: I am often reminded of him helping people no matter what, and at any time. What stands out the most is how he dedicated himself to helping to take care of his sick mother for a number of years.

Q: If there were something you could say to him or share about Craig today, what would that be?

A: Craig was the most mechanically inclined person I've ever met and had the widest range of friends. He had friends of all races and backgrounds and spent quality time with all of them. And if he liked you and you asked him for help he would never, ever leave you hanging. He always helped you.

Chapter 6
QUIERRA WELLS

Quierra—Tony's daughter and my granddaughter—was the inspiration for my first book titled *To Quierra, On Life*. When Craig and I married, Quierra, was about two. Craig knew how much my first grandchild meant to me. He embraced her with as much love and affection as if she were his own grandchild. He used to boast about how he was the only one who could stop her crying, especially when she would be at the top of her crying episodes with a pitch that could break any crystal glass nearby. Craig would imitate her crying which seemed to work every time in getting her to stop. He also used to sing her name loudly: "Quierra!" which always brought sniggles from her each time he would do that. As Quierra continued to grow, she spent many weekends with Craig and me. When we bought our homes in Maryland and West Virginia, Quierra was always spending time with us, along with my nephews (her cousins). Craig loved helping to entertain them with hiking, fishing, and exploring.

Quierra and I went on many vacations throughout the years. Some with Craig and some without. We surprised Quierra with her first cruise when she graduated from high school. It only seemed natural that during my last vacation with Craig, which was a cruise, Quierra, was also sharing the time with us. Quierra has expressed the following thoughts...

Q: What would you say about the title of the book in regards to Craig?

A: It sounds like something Craig would say. It's a pretty good quote; he had a great philosophy on life. I admired that about him.

Q: Do you remember your first conversations about Craig after learning of his diagnosis?

A: I called my cousin Romel crying because I didn't want it to be true. I remember being both sad and upset with him because I thought he would always be around. He just seemed like one of those people built to last, like Ford cars, ha ha. But seriously, I never imagined him falling victim to a disease. He was too strong for that. But over time, I accepted it. I still miss him very much.

Q: What was your response and reaction to the news?

A: I was driving and pulled over and spoke to Romel about it. It was very hard. I think Craig actually called me and told me which made it harder, but the strength in his voice carried me through the conversation.

Q: How often did you have the opportunity to spend time with him?

A: Often enough to make an unforgettable impact on my life. He took Devin and Chris, and probably Bree, and me, canoeing, which was something a bunch of black kids in Baltimore rarely had the opportunity to do. We also went fishing a lot when we were younger. That's what I loved about Craig; he always introduced us to something new.

Q: How has your life changed or been impacted while visiting and talking with him in his final days?

A: The best time we spent together was when was went on our last vacation on the cruise to the Bahamas. It was an exceptional experience. This was the first time I ever actually got to see him cry or show raw emotion. It was during a play, or a show on the cruise ship. I can't remember the play or the song, but it was an emotional moment. My grandmother might remember it though. Craig seemed to have a really good time on this trip. The one thing that I really remember is that he had a very, very huge appetite. One night he ate two large lobster tails, one right after the other. We left him at the table eating. He ate a lot for as small as he was.

Craig was determined to live his life to the fullest, especially when the doctors told him he had twenty days left to live. How can they tell someone they have twenty days to live anyway? Craig lived his life like he didn't believe it because he kept right on going. It's like he didn't believe them. His attitude was, "It's my life and it is my time and nobody is going to tell me what to do with it."

Craig had a huge impact on my appreciation for good food. He was a great cook and he introduced me to great food. I developed a very discriminating palate. I love good food and so did he.

Q: If there were something you could say or share with Craig today, what would that be?

A: I would thank him for giving me good advice on what I should look for in a GOOD man. He set up my expectations for what a good man should be. Can he cook? Is he a handyman? He has to be handy and able to fix things, because Craig could fix anything. He set the example and gave me high expectations for the type of men or what kind of men I would meet as well as what I should be concerned about in all areas of my life. For this, Craig, I will forever be grateful to you.

Chapter 7
CHRISTOPHER JONES

Christopher was Craig's Godson and nephew. I met Craig through my sister Dee Dee's previous husband. Craig and Kevin were students together at a RETS technical school. They were both in between careers, in search of a profession that would bring them better job opportunities. I am told that when Craig saw a picture of me from Dee Dee and Kevin's wedding, Craig remarked, "Who was that sexy, silver-haired lady? I would like to meet her." Kevin replied to Craig, "That's my sister-in-law, Cookie, but she's too *wild* for you." I was told by Craig that he begged to meet me for months to my sister Dee Dee, and the rest is history.

Through Kevin and Dee Dee's union, two sons were born. When Craig learned of the second son, he asked to be the Godfather, so Dee Dee and Kevin agreed. I believe Christopher's first name is from Craig's middle name, which delighted Craig so much. He felt such a connection with Christopher, even until the very last day of his living. Chris could do no wrong. He was the son Craig never had. By not having any children, Craig felt he could fascinate Chris with his many tales of adventure. On the final day of Craig's passing away, family came to the hospital to see him. At that time, Chris, Devin-my other nephew, and Dee Dee, were making their way to West Virginia. I remembered sitting on the side of the bed with Craig, noticing that his breathing had become very shallow. His eyes never opened, but I leaned forward, kissed him on the forehead and said to him, "Baby, Chris is on his way."

Craig continued to breathe slowly. He did not seem to want the oxygen anymore. His eyes remained closed. Chris and family finally arrived around 10:00 a.m. Chris went right to Craig's bed and sat on its side. He had a private, quiet, conversation with Craig; he held his hand for a while and when he quietly got up, he had tears in his eyes. I am not sure exactly where Chris went, as the hospital room was a little crowded by then with us all. But I do remember looking over at Craig to check on his breathing after Chris left his side. It was about 10:15. Craig was no longer breathing. Was he truly waiting for Chris to say his goodbyes, the only *son* he'd known? Hmm, not the first time I had heard others speak of a similar experience with their loved ones. Here is what Chris had to say about his God-dad.

Q: What would you say about the title of the book in regards to Craig?

A: I recall specifically my mother and Aunt Cookie talking about how Craig was in pain and that he was ready to be at peace with it all. After hearing them talk about how he would be pissed if he woke up the next day, I knew that Craig would be ready to move on. It all started to hit me that his battle with cancer was coming to an end, and he had enough courage and pride to admit that. I recalled talking to Craig in the hospital months before he actually passed away, and how he talked about how he wanted to do everything to stay alive. He truly did put up a good fight, but at the end, after trying different approaches to curing his cancer, watching his family come by and surrounding him with love, he decided to come to his peace. Towards the end, he seemed very uncomfortable, and in a lot of pain, and seemed as if all he wanted was for the pain to go away. He did not want to wake up tomorrow in the pain he was in.

Q: Do you remember your first conversation with Craig after learning of his diagnosis?

A: I recall this pretty vividly. It was shortly after my other uncle, Michael Chandler, passed away. I remember thinking to myself about how heartbreaking it was that two uncles were diagnosed with cancer in such a close period of time from one another. I, of course, had a tremendous amount of hope that he would get past this. Like the Sagittarian spirit in myself, I knew that Craig was not going to go through cancer without a fight, and that he would do everything to overcome the disease. He fought a good fight for a very long time, and even so, continued to be very cheerful, insightful, optimistic, and funny throughout it all.

Q: What was your response and reaction to the news?

A: I was just very shocked about it all. I had a lot of questions, started wondering why and how he got the cancer. I knew that Craig was a heavy smoker, but I never thought he would have cancer. I also recall receiving a phone call from my Aunt Cookie when I was working the overnight shift. My Aunt Cookie was in tears, panicking that the cancer was ultimately getting ready to take over Craig. She gave the phone to Craig and I began to cry thanking him for being a great godfather and uncle. He chuckled and said that everything was okay right then and that, "I'm not checking out now." This made me relax, eventually going back to work, but still starting to get very consumed with the news about the cancer.

Q: How often did you have the opportunity to spend time with him?

A: Not often enough. I did come to the hospital with my mother a few times. Probably about five times, had a few conversations with him on the phone, but of course not as often as I wish I had.

Q: How has your life changed or been impacted while visiting and talking with him in his final days?

A: I honestly never had to deal with death until the death of Craig. Having Craig pass away was very difficult because he was also a friend to me. Visiting and watching him in the bed while sick is something that I try to erase from my mind. I will never forget in his last moment, I walked over to Craig and said, "Thank you. Now get some rest." Less than a minute later, Craig was gone. I felt like he passed in peace knowing that his family and friends loved him dearly, and he had so much love around him.

Q: What are your fondest memories of Craig?

A: As I mentioned at the funeral, Craig was definitely like a second father to me. I am laughing as I write this, thinking about how he used to always tell everyone that he gave me my first bath. Craig was the ideal godfather. I remember at the age of seven, calling Craig asking him to help me build a go-cart. Craig was someone who used to tell me stories—

thousands of them—while riding in his many white vans through the hills of West Virginia. In my eyes, Craig knew everything. He let me drive his white van at only ten years old. He showed me how to fish, scared the hell out of me with the live worms, and took me on my first roller coaster ride at Disney World. I have so many memories with Craig. He enjoyed having me as a godson, and I'm very lucky to have had such a bond with someone who was so intelligent, so cool, and so wise. One of the greatest moments I ever had with Craig was when he took me to West Virginia for my thirteenth birthday and we went hiking. We walked five miles and he was shocked that I didn't get tired one bit. My mind was too focused on the different views, tunnels, lakes, and mountains that he showed me along the way to be tired. I remember him taking me on the very top of the mountain and showing me how Maryland, Virginia, and West Virginia all connected in one view. It's one I will never forget.

Q: If there was something you could say or share with Craig today, what would that be?

A: I would just share with Craig that he has definitely been a huge influence on my life. I have this love for the outdoors because of Craig. Every time I go hiking, fishing, or drive the huge hills of West Virginia, I will always think of him. Love you, God-dad!

PART III

CONVERSATIONS WITH FRIENDS

Throughout the course of our marriage, Craig had many friends, some more interesting than others. The majority of his friendships lasted until his passing. When Craig became your friend, you had a friend for life. There was no line of demarcation between my friends and his, so he thought. In other words, my friends were his friends, but to me, his friends were *his* friends. I kept the boundaries a little more distinctive than he did. Craig was the person you called for any situation, no matter night or day. I had to accept this over time. But this time, he called and they came. And when I called, they also came. Here are some of the conversations and their remembrances.

Chapter 8
STAN AND MARY PALMER

I am not certain as to who coined the phrase "people are in our lives for a reason, a season, or maybe a lifetime." What I do know is that Stan and Mary were definitely there for us in our season. I can't imagine how we could have gotten through this experience without them.

Craig loved "his Stan." They met at a time when Craig worked for a home improvement company in the Baltimore metro area. Even though Craig had phenomenal skills in the home improvement area, he worked as a subcontractor for another contractor; he did that for the security of steady employment. When Stan recognized Craig's craftsmanship, he encouraged Craig to branch out on his own, and he did. From that conversation, a friendship grew that lasted until he passed away about ten years later.

Stan was so patient with Craig. They had many tales throughout their friendship that could make another book. When Craig and I moved to West Virginia, we often housed at Stan and Mary's, who were often away flying somewhere. They were both private pilots. It was a "win-win" situation for us all. So, it was only natural that the call to Stan was probably the second or third call made when Craig learned of his diagnosis. They were both so kind and understanding to us both, and so concerned when he was told them that he had little time left. Stan insisted that we stay in their home during the radiation and chemotherapy treatments.

The idea of meeting someone who was a private pilot was so exciting and unbelievable to Craig. And yes, Stan did teach Craig how to fly. He used to come home so enthused about his flying trips with Stan! About two weeks before Craig made the decision to stay at home in West Virginia and no longer travel back and forth to Baltimore, he made one final flight with Stan. This expedition was one episode of a week of "final adventures" for Craig. He also went crabbing in the bay with his friend Smitty, something he had long wanted to do. I could tell now that his energy level was becoming low. He was getting tired now physically, but he was still upbeat mentally.

Stan, Mary, and Stan's son came to see Craig the Friday before he passed away at the hospital in West Virginia. The conversations were limited. However, I do remember Stan saying something to Craig like, "You don't have to keep fighting." And then he added, "It's okay to let go." I also remember him asking Craig to send him a sign, some kind of sign so that he would know that he was okay. That's how deep their friendship was.

Craig seemed to enjoy the exercises that Stan's son was doing with his legs. They looked so thin and were becoming cold to the touch. Still, the bending of them back and forth brought some comfort in his bed. His legs were no longer supporting him. When Stan, Mary, and their son left, Craig followed them out with his eyes, affixed on Mary who was crying. He appeared to want to say to her "don't' cry", but he just silently watched them all leave. He knew it would be their last time with him. Here is some of what Stan had to say about his friend...

Q: What would you say about the title of the book as it relates to Craig?

A: So true of Craig, the title. I've never seen someone with such determination to beat the cancer, knowing the odds were against him.

Q: Do you remember your first conversation with Craig after learning of his diagnosis?

A: Yes, he said, "I was diagnosed with lung cancer, and it's not good."

Q: What was your response and reaction to the news?

A: I was so sad, as Mary was, and feared we would soon lose such a dear friend.

Q: How often did you have the opportunity to spend time with him?

A: A lot. I regret that he didn't accept my offer to go flying gliders with me in Nevada. He wanted to finish a job at work. We became friends when he installed new windows in our house in 1996.

Q: How has your life changed or been impacted while visiting and talking with him in his final days?

A: I am still in awe of the courage he showed with this two-plus year battle. I think of him almost every day and laugh at our past adventures, specifically flying the remote gliders, fishing, and admiring his skill as a master carpenter. He had a new story or crisis every day we spoke. We had some wild adventures, such as taking a motorboat out to a shipwreck and diving for treasure! Then our battery died and the engine wouldn't start and we drifted ashore where Mary brought a new battery. Craig portaged the battery on his head out to the boat. This trip took three hours in ten-foot waves at forty degree temperatures with only t-shirts and shorts on!

Fortunately, he did join us in Montana. Yvonne has his picture on the wall in the hunting camp lodge. The first black man on the ranch! He was well received. Craig always jumped at the chance to go flying with me. We did acrobatic flight maneuvers, the air cam open cockpit, and many other small planes like Cessnas, RV's, Paris jet...

Q: If there is something you could say or share with Craig today, what would that be?

A: Before he died, we made a pact for him to signal me that 'all is well', wherever he's at. I haven't received his signal, but will be on lookout!

About a year or so ago, I received an email from Stan and Mary with a photograph attached. The photograph showed a picture of a falcon (bird) sitting on the wing of a small plane they were flying; the plane was thousands of miles in the air. They were both amazed as to how this bird could still be positioned on this plane at such a high altitude; they could not believe how stoic it looked. It then hit them like the flash of a lighten bolt! They believed it was the sign that they had been waiting for. They believe, and I believe too, that it was Craig letting his best friend know that he did not forget his promise to let him know that he was "okay." Nothing exemplifies Craig more than the strong and steady grasp of a falcon.

Chapter 9
SHERRIE BISHOP

Sherrie is one of the sweetest and kindest persons one could ever meet. But this was not my initial perception of her. I could not "get with" this relationship between her and Craig. I can remember Craig's coming home enamored by the new "tile girl" that Charlie—owner of Accurate Builders, the employer of them both—had hired. Sherrie worked on and off with Craig and his crew; she was one of the boys. It would have been very befitting if Sherrie looked like one who could be on her knees all day installing tile. But no, she didn't, so when there is a pretty new face that comes on the scene in any job place, the boys tend to act like high school students who want to get the pretty girl's attention. And, yes, Craig seemed to be the one who got most of her attention. So the green-eyed monster in me became very suspicious in the beginning. And the two of them did seem to have more in common than he and I did. As stated earlier, I had to learn to accept all of Craig's friends, and they were from all walks of life. So, reluctantly, when Craig asked me to join him to see Sherrie perform (yes, she could sing too), I acquiesced and went with him.

I remember her first reaction in meeting me. I didn't know what she was expecting, but she said to Craig, "You didn't tell me she was a hottie!" We laughed and this broke the ice between us. From then on, Craig and Sherrie became very close. He would come home upset a lot about what she was going through in her relationship with her significant other. But that was Craig, always taking on other people's problems and bringing them home to me to have to listen to sometimes all night. And when it was after a couple of beers, I would be in for a long night. I became very good at faking sleep.

When Craig's mom became very ill, Sherrie was there for Craig. She would listen to how hurt he was in seeing his mom in her last days of life. Sherrie even provided assistance when Craig needed someone to stay with his mom when there were other schedule conflicts. When Craig became ill, Sherrie was there for him as well. He seemed so comforted by the knowledge that she was taking this journey with him. They even had conversations about where he wanted his ashes to be scattered—in the lake directly behind where we resided. Sherrie would often visit with Craig in that final month before he passed, while I worked. By that time Sherrie had remarried and her husband understood the depth of their friendship.

The Friday of the weekend before Craig passed away, I was putting a plan in place to be at home with him all the time. Sherrie borrowed my SUV so that she could make the trip back and forth. Craig never allowed anyone to borrow any of our vehicles; yet he had no objections during that time. On my way home that Friday, I received a call from Sherrie. She stated that Craig was insisting that she call 911 so he could go to the hospital. Craig was home under hospice care, and I felt that going to the hospital via ambulance would not be in his best interest.

I asked Sherrie to let me speak to Craig. When Sherrie gave Craig the phone, he started speaking in a loud voice to me, "NINE ONE ONE."

I asked, "Honey, what's wrong, why do you want 911?"

He responded, "Have her call 911!"

I said, "Okay. I'm on my way, but put Sherrie back on the phone." When Sherrie got back on the phone I advised her to call 911 as he wanted, and I informed her that I would meet her at City Hospital in Martinsburg, WV. I also advised her not to argue with him, even in his final days, as he could still be like a stubborn mule.

When I got to the hospital, Craig was just arriving by ambulance. After all of the preliminaries, he was finally put in a room. This was not our first stay there, so his medical status was already known. Sherrie stayed with us through the night. Friday went into Saturday and family and friends began to come one by one. That Saturday night, we all talked and had some light-hearted conversations. Craig would drift in and out of sleep. During that night, Sherrie helped Craig maneuver in the bed. As she was helping him to get comfortable, she stated to me something that I will never forget. As she was pulling him up to a comfortable position, he whispered in her ear, "If I wake up tomorrow, I'm gonna be pissed." Here are some of Sherrie's thoughts…

Q: What would you say about the title of the book as it relates to Craig?

A: I like it. It's appropriate for him.

Q: Why do you think it's appropriate?

A: Because the night before he died, he said, "If I wake up tomorrow, I'm gonna be pissed."

Q: And why do you think he said that?

A: Because he was miserable and in pain and tired of fighting.

Q: Do you remember your first conversations with Craig after his diagnosis?

A: I remember some conversations with him. He actually was having a hard time dealing with you (Cookie) being sick at the same time. He was more concerned with you than he was with himself. I remember that.

Q: What was your response or reaction to the news?

A: I was sad, heartbroken, and hopeful that it was going to pass. He had a lot of hope. So I've never seen anyone recover from lung cancer. I wasn't hopeful by myself, I was only hopeful because he was hopeful.

Q: How often did you have the opportunity to spend time with him?

A: It was not a lot of time, but it was quality time. We walked around the lake around your house in West Virginia. He said how he wanted to have his ashes scattered on that island over there, not in the water. And he asked me not to leave him because he knew he was going to die.

Q: How has your life changed or been impacted by the loss of such a good friend?

A: Craig died during a time when I was losing a lot of people in my life. Everybody was dying all at once. And he died on my aunt's birthday. I was glad that I was able to be there at the end because he asked me to be there. I would have felt bad if I wasn't able to. And I was glad that I got his brother Drake to stay that night too because he wouldn't have been there.

He was actually the first friend that I lost, ever. So I guess it feels like how anyone would feel who has lost such a good friend for the first time.

Q: What were some of your fondest memories of Craig?

A: He was a hillbilly, the first black cowboy I ever met, and he took me to the first country bar I ever went to. He took me there a few times, and he was well-known, well-liked. We drank and smoked a lot together. And he loved country music. He could drink and drive like nobody's business. I worried and worried, but he never got into an accident. I used to wonder how he had a wife who would go out and be so independent, yet he remained so confident and happy. It was a nice way that people could be together and not be so co-dependent. That taught me a lot about relationships.

Q: If there were something you could say or share with Craig today, what would that be?

A: I would say I got married and it will be three years this September. I have grandchildren too!

Chapter 10
TOM BEAUCHAMP

I had the opportunity to meet Tom and his wife before Craig and I married. We visited their home in the Eastern Shore/Pocomoke City area. At that time, they were in the process of building their new home. Craig and Tom were two of a kind when it came to their love of beer. Craig was so proud of his friend; he had become very successful in the construction arena. Craig met Tom when he resided in Baltimore years ago and their friendship continued until his death. When we got married, Tom was there, and I think he celebrated more than the both of us! It might have been because we had to borrow money to have the elaborate wedding that Craig wanted. This was Craig's first marriage, and funny enough, to a "sistah," much to some of his friends' surprise, including Tom, at least that's what Craig said.

Craig and Tom stayed in contact with each other throughout the years. When Tom and his wife Peggy bought their RV, Craig and I had the pleasure of spending time with them. It was my first time ever camping at a campsite in an RV, and that site was near our home in West Virginia. Craig and I talked about how much fun we had with Tom, his wife, and other friends for a long time after that. Craig always seemed to be loved by the wives of his friends. Craig was just as pleased talking and spending time with Peggy as he was with Tom.

So I knew that Tom had to be in the top five calls made by Craig when he learned of his cancer diagnosis. And once again, as with the others, Tom and Peggy came. Not just once, but as I recall, a couple of times to be with their friend.

Each time they came, Craig seemed to always be excited and happy to be with them. During one of the last visits, they took us out to dinner. Craig did not have much of an appetite due to the effects of his chemo treatments. His tongue was very sore from the thrush.

Still they insisted, and we made the best of that time with each other. We received a beautiful hourglass from Tom and Peggy during his last days. I am not quite sure what precipitated their buying Craig this gift; however, when he opened it, his face lit up like a child's. This hourglass, filled with purple sand, still sits on my living room table. Tom expressed the following thoughts...

Q: What would you say about the title of the book in regards to Craig?

A: Very interesting. The first part, The Courage to Die and the Spirit to Live, is very Craig as is the second half ("And If I Wake Up Tomorrow, I'm Gonna Be Pissed) is even more Craig. He would love it.

Q: Do you remember your first conversations with Craig after learning of his diagnosis?

A: Yes, he was very upbeat and confident, said he could deal with it, and the cancer hospital he was going to in Philadelphia really made him feel special. They would pick him up in a limo and put him up in a fancy hotel and feed him fine food.

Q: What was your response and reaction to the news?

A: Sadness.

Q: How often did you have the opportunity to spend time with him?

A: Only about three or four times.

Q: How has your life changed or been impacted by visiting and talking with him in his final days?

A: Craig was one of those people you meet and he becomes a lifelong trusted friend and that in itself changes your life. Him passing made me very sad.

Q: What are some of your fondest memories of Craig?

A: Craig was a very special friend. I met him while I was going to Towson State in 1971. We had rented an apartment off of Cold Spring Lane where Craig, Drake, and his mother lived. Anyway, while we were moving in, I was walking up the stairs and dropped my "special" roller. Craig picked it up, smiled, and when he handed it back, he said I didn't need that thing, he could teach me how to roll by hand; remember, he was only twelve years old. From that day forward, we created a bond of friendship and trust which lasted forty-one years.

Q: If there were something you could say or share with Craig today, what would that be?

A: Well, if he were here, we would get on the phone and spend at least an hour catching up. We would share old stories, talk about what new toys we each had, and talk about when I was coming up to take him on that special Gold Wing motorcycle ride.

Chapter 11
DAVE AND JENNY SPECTOR

Dave and Jenny Spector were friends before Craig and I met. My recollection from Craig was that they'd met when Dave and Craig's brother Drake were attending Drexel University in Delaware. Craig would visit his brother and during that time, he befriended Dave too. That would be typical of Craig; he wanted to be friends with everybody else's friends. It was a good union in spite of their religious differences: Jewish and Catholic. These differences never seemed to matter to Craig or his family. His friends were so diverse! Craig, Dave, and Drake continued their friendships throughout the years. Dave and his wife Jenny also attended our wedding.

Both Dave and Craig teamed up together and subcontracted with Accurate Builders until David branched out on his own. Craig worked with David for a period of time; however, two perfectionists are not always the best working partners. Craig would come home not in the best of moods after a day's work with Dave. Craig was always so sensitive to any type of criticism, constructive or not, from anyone. But the relationship was never impacted by work conflicts. They continued to remain friends, and both Dave and Jenny came through for us in the end. I always had a fondness of Jenny, but it was her encouraging words and prayers that helped us both during this season. I still have the prayer blanket she made for us. Here is what Dave and Jenny had to say about their journey with Craig.

Q: What would you say about the title of the book in regards to Craig?

A: I think the title of the book is perfect, and I truly believe Craig was smiling when he heard it.

Q: Do you remember your first conversations with Craig after learning of his diagnosis?

A: My memory is slowly leaving me, but I do remember Craig

calling and I think it was the month of May, but as always, when he would call and I answered the phone, he would ask in a deep voice, "Is it safe to talk?" That would always make me laugh. David was not home the night he called and we talked for a while. He was very upfront about the cancer and had a very positive attitude.

Q: How often did you have the opportunity to spend time with him?

A: I wish that we were able to spend more time with him, but whenever we got together, he was always upbeat. At least around me.

Q: What are some of your fondest memories of Craig?

A: One of my fondest memories is when he came up to see me and spent the night. We had a claw foot tub and he loved taking a bath in it. My concern was that he would fall asleep. I remember having David check on him. I didn't want him to drown.

Q: If there were something you could say or share with Craig today, what would that be?

A: That he would always hold a special place in our hearts.

Chapter 12
ROBIN AND MICHELE SPECTOR

Robin was the brother of Dave Spector. I remember meeting Robin and Michele for the first time at their wedding. They had begun to build on their new home in the Baltimore County area. It was such a beautiful, yet simple, wedding held in their back yard. As I understand it, Craig became friends with Robin during the same time he and Dave met. This was also during Craig's brother Drake and Robin's brother Dave's, college years. And as already stated, it never mattered to Craig how he became one's friend; a first or second meeting would be enough for him to attach himself to claim you as his friend. Robin and Craig had many things in common as well. And he would often visit them throughout the years. When we bought our home in West Virginia, Robin was always a welcomed guest for Craig, as they both loved fishing in the lake.

I used to run into Michele from time to time in downtown Baltimore. I always thought of her as being very kind and friendly. When they opened their restaurant in downtown Baltimore, Craig and I enjoyed going there to eat. We were so impressed with Robin's food acumen! That too was something the two of them shared.

When Craig branched out on his own in the home improvement field, he would call on Robin to do the painting. Robin was as meticulous in this craft as Craig was in the carpentry area. When Robin and Michele moved into their beautiful new home, Craig was right there making sure no wool had been pulled over their eyes. Another indication of being needed! It only seemed a natural question to ask Craig if he had shared with Robin the news of his illness. He told me he would be letting him know soon. I am not sure as to when he did inform him, but I do know that Robin and Michele came to offer their support as well. Here is some of what they shared.

Q: What would you say about the cover of the book regarding Craig?

A-Robin: Yes, Craig was a most spirited fellow.

A-Michele: I like it, but maybe instead of 'I'm going to be pissed', possibly 'I'm Going to Be Pissed I Didn't Finish My Bucket List).

Q: Do you remember your first conversations about Craig after learning of his diagnosis?

A-Robin: I found the news of Craig's diagnosis shocking and saddening.

A-Michele: My memory of my conversation consisted of how bad I felt for him and how bad the diagnosis was, but also how courageous and determined Craig was with his battle with cancer. I also admired how he continued to work, driving all that way from West Virginia to Baltimore. He also talked openly about a bucket list. I often wondered if he got to check some of them off. I couldn't remember the list but I am sure he talked about it.

Q: What was your response and reaction to the news?

A-Robin: From my similar experience with my own mother, I knew the prognosis was bleak. I tried to be as upbeat as possible for Craig.

A-Michele: I was shocked and had a deep sadness for this gentle man who always made me smile. I remember thinking that he was way too young for lung cancer and I felt it just wasn't fair. I remember praying for him.

Q: How often did you have the opportunity to spend time with him?

A-Robin: After Craig's diagnosis, I spent more time [with him] than ever before. I found him coming to my home frequently for friendship and support and I found myself visiting him as often as possible.

A-Michele: I remember Rob and I and the kids visiting him in their house in West Virginia and fishing in the lake. It was a day that will always be in my box of memories of Craig. He was very open about his diagnosis and I remember trying to be encouraging. He really loved that house and it showed. Fairly often, he would stop by our house in Baltimore while Cookie was teaching, and visit with our family. It was always good to see him. He was almost always smiling and cracking jokes as usual. His complaints were few, and occasionally he would sit on the sofa and take a little snooze. He said the medicine knocked him out.

Q: How has your life changed or been impacted while visiting and talking with him in his final days?

A-Robin: Only to say that spending so much time with him in his final days did bring me closure. I truly miss him and think of him often.

A-Michele: It made me realize that things can happen and change your life drastically. I saw how much courage and strength Craig had. It also provoked conversation with Rob about how smoking can destroy a life. I thought of how Craig quit smoking and how easy it was when faced with such news. I know how much willpower it takes to quit after smoking thirty years. A couple of years ago Rob quit smoking and he says it was the hardest thing he has ever done. I think Craig had a big influence on that decision and I thank him for that. I think he [Craig] would be proud of that.

Q: What were some of your fondest memories of Craig?

A-Robin: I think two of my fondest memories of Craig both involved fishing; us fishing together. The first was years ago returning from a long early morning fishing trip on Liberty Reservoir. As we were headed to the boat dock, Craig had left his fishing line in the water. In the interim, he had also fallen asleep, so when a fish hit his line the look of shock and surprise was quite hilarious. We both chuckled over that many times. The second was our grand success fishing at the mini-lake in West Virginia just after his diagnosis. I had brought some very large bait grubs, and it was the first time he or I had ever used such bait. It seemed some very large bluegills were willing to suck them down like candy. It felt really good to have a mutually uplifting experience with

Craig. I also have fond memories of just hanging out at Craig's apartment at Bonnie Ridge. Whether it was listening to Craig speak fondly of Drake or his mom, whom it seemed everyone had a love thing for because she was just so sweet; or talk about crazy Mike, the big white cat, or Kevin Carter, a mutual friend, we enjoyed each other's company.

A-Michele: I met Craig through Rob and remember how easy it was to converse with him. He had a way of making you feel comfortable and usually made you smile. He had a gentle, calming voice and always seemed so cool, calm, and collected no matter what was going on. I will always remember his great sense of humor. I may not have seen him often, but when I did, it wasn't hard to catch up on our daily lives. He always talked about his nieces, nephews, and grandchildren. You could tell how much he cared for them. He had a good relationship with his wife and often praised all of her milestones. He was proud that she had retired from her lifelong job, had two doctorates, and was a college professor. He was a true family man. One fond memory I will always cherish is that he caught the garter at my and Rob's wedding. Even more fond memories include being invited to the annual family parties at his brother Drake's house. It was always nice to see everyone, especially Craig. He always made you feel comfortable.

Q: If there were something you could say or share with Craig today, what would that be?

A-Robin: "Craig, man, I don't have many friends, and I truly considered you one of them. I loved you like a brother. If you could, please send me the answers to all the unanswered questions I have. Here's to you, Bro. I hope you are in a good place. Lemme know, will ya? I miss you."

A-Michele: I would say, "Craig, I am so thankful to have shared all those times and conversations with you, and when I think of you I can still hear your gentle voice and see your great smile. You will never be forgotten. I hope you are looking down and smiling in your heart."

Chapter 13
RAY JOHNSON

"Ray" was a blessing in our lives; Divine Timing is how Craig and I saw him. At the time Craig and Ray met, Ray had been assisting me as my financial consultant. He was referred to me by my best friend Val. After Ray was convinced that Craig was as skillful in the home improvement arena as he stated himself to be, they teamed up together and a business as well as a good friendship evolved, lasting until Craig was no longer able to work.

Ray would allow Craig to bring his own help to work on the many projects around the Baltimore metro area, and one such person was my son Tony. Ray trusted Craig to get the job done and he trusted the people he brought to do it. That's how Craig was; he always had a desire to teach his craft and bring employment to anyone who needed to be employed, and oftentimes, right away. Unfortunately, Craig's desire to help at times brought him grief because his *help* did not always have the skillset needed, which meant he could not meet his deadlines. So needless to say, I had to hear all about how inept some of his help was, but he still kept them on, and would take them out for a 'cold one' on him after work! He never gave up on anyone. One of my better memories of this relationship was a huge deck that Craig single-handedly built for Ray in between other jobs when Ray bought a new home. It was the largest deck I had ever seen. Ray was even kind enough to allow me to have my granddaughter's twenty-first birthday celebration there. Everyone was so in awe of that deck!

When Craig could no longer be productive in meeting the needs of the business, Ray still allowed him to come to the job site and share his knowledge from a consulting perspective and be paid. He got to know Ray's family well. He would come home and share conversations about Ray's mom and dad, his sister—Ms. Johnson as he referred to her—and Ray's nephews who worked with him daily.

The call to let Ray know of Craig's passing was hard for me. For a while they had not spoken as Craig was going back and forth to treatments and had been hospitalized as well. When he had his final conversation with Ray, he seemed quite content in knowing that it would be his last conversation with him, and it was a good conversation. Here is what Ray shared about his journey with Craig.

Q: What would you say about the title of the book in regards to Craig?

A: I think it's a catchy title. It is a catchy title because it will make you think. It sounds just like Craig.

Q: Can you remember the first conversation you had with Cookie or Craig about his diagnosis?

A: Yes, I was the person that made him go to the doctor. He had this lingering cough, and he kept saying it was a cold, and making one excuse after another. Until one day on the job site, I noticed how winded he was trying to make it up a flight of steps. He couldn't do it, he just didn't seem his normal self to me, so I made him go home from the job site. And I told him to make an appointment for the doctor, or I was going to call Cookie, so he made the appointment.

Q: How often did you meet with him during this time?

A: I met with him almost every day. Even when he was diagnosed and could not work any longer. He would come down to the job site and supervise, just so he could keep his mind off of his illness. The guys still made him feel like a part of the crew and did what they could to keep his spirits up.

Q: What are your fondest memories of Craig?

A: He was a multi-tasker. He was a man of many talents and hobbies. He had some of the strangest habits for a black guy. He did stuff most black people didn't do, and he ate things that black people didn't eat. I mean, one day he came in here with chicken feet and he ate squirrel and all kinds strange things. When he told me he needed time off to get his pilot's license, I didn't believe him, because how many black people do you know get their pilot's license? We called him "little MacGyver" because he could fix or do anything. He was a pilot, a mechanic, he was good at so many things. I had known Cookie for a long time before I met Craig. I wish I had met him sooner, because he did such good work, and I could trust him with my business. I happened to mention to her one day that I was looking for a contractor. Do you know how many of my clients have come in here and said their husbands were contractors or that they knew a good contractor? Well, Cookie told me her husband was in home improvements, and I thought sure, and she had told me this about four years before I met him.

Q: How has your life changed or been impacted while visiting and talking with him in his final days?

A: He helped me grow my business. We probably worked on at least fifteen jobs, and I think we probably worked on more houses than that together. This house was the last house we worked on for me. He helped me make my business what it is today and he was very much a part of my everyday life. It took me a minute to get back on my feet after he passed because it took me a while to find somebody I could trust like I trusted him. I trusted him with my life. I helped him move from Owings Mills back to West Virginia, so we did a lot of things together. He stayed at my house when he was too ill to travel back and forth to West Virginia. He was a good man.

Q: If you could say or share something with him today, what would that be?

A: I would have a 'cold one' with him and take him to Vegas. We never got to go to Las Vegas. At the end of the work day, he and I, along with the crew, would finish up with sharing a six-pack or two, and that's what I would do again if I could. (Smile)

Chapter 14
PINKY PATEL

Pinky was our "angel" in the midst of this challenge. We met during the time we both worked for Genesis Healthcare at Catonsville Commons. I don't even remember how our friendship evolved to the level that it has; but she was truly there for Craig and me throughout the entire time. I do remember that I could hardly understand anything she said during our first years of being employed together. I came on board there as the Social Services Director. She was first a nurse then became what I called the "money maker" functioning as our clinical reimbursement coordinator. I never met anyone who on one hand had a heart of gold, but get on her wrong side, or be inept in your work responsibilities, and she would chew you up and spit you out in a split second!

I used to tell her that I always thought women from her country of India were passive and meek in their demeanor. We would often laugh when I stated her gene pool must have crossed up with maybe our "sister-girl" gene pool, cuz girlfriend took no stuff off of anyone! My days at Genesis, Catonsville Commons, however, led to a family of great friends and acquaintances that continue until this day. Our hurts, disappointments, joy, and laughter are all shared. The news of Craig's illness was one that really affected us all, and when Pinky learned about it, she wanted to be there for us. Like a 'sistah', she did not mince her words with me; she told me that lung cancer is a very mean and painful form of cancer. She told me I would be going through a rough time. But she also told me that no matter what, she would be there for us.

Craig really loved Pinky too. We would always "crack-up," as all of us from the work force would, whenever she tried to correctly use the vernacular. I tried so hard in helping her get it right, but it was to no avail! Pinky's family became mine and my family became hers. Craig felt comfortable with her clinical knowledge, so having her on his final vacation cruise was very reassuring to him. He knew

The Courage to Die with the Spirit to Live

he would be in good hands and he was. Here is the conversation shared by Pinky.

Q – What would you say about the title of the book in regards to Craig?

A: The title is appropriate for the book because the evening before he passed, "if I wake up tomorrow, I'm gonna be pissed" was his last response. He asked for help to sit on the edge of the bed and after that he did not get up anymore.

Q: Can you remember the first conversation you had with Craig about his diagnosis?

A: Craig never really personally verbalized to me that he had cancer or that he was dying. The only conversation that we had about his diagnosis was on the cruise a month before he passed. He expressed that he was afraid and concerned for Cookie about the way she was seeing him suffering. He was more concerned about the fact that Cookie was watching him suffer. I said to him, "You know, Craig, Cookie is strong and you should not be worried about her and we will take care of her. I will always be with her and she will never be alone."

Q: How often were you able to spend time or visit with him during this time?

A: I had the opportunity to stay with him in West Virginia and at my apartment before he passed away to help Cookie take care of him so that she could adjust her work schedule. During this time, he was getting weaker and weaker and needed help to perform his daily functions. I was able to assist him with his daily functions and medical care. I could tell he was mentally worrying about Cookie and my message to him was not to worry, just to take care of yourself and rest and be comfortable to take this journey. She will be okay.

Q: How was your life changed or been impacted while visiting and talking with him during his final days?

A: Seeing him live life to the fullest, especially joining him and Cookie on the cruise to Bermuda, was a blessing. Watching him eat until he was full, seeing him drink a sixteen-ounce frosted beer, and having a good time dancing under the stars until the early morning light. To live life just like him to the fullest. That is what I learned.

Q: What is your fondest memory of Craig?

A: My fondest memory of Craig is his unconditional love that he had for Cookie and his friends, and what a wonderful person he was with everyone he met and with everyone he was around.

Q: If you could share or say anything to him today, what would that be?

A: If I could share or say anything to him today, I would tell him, "I told you so! Cookie is okay, she has you looking after her from above, and always will. I will always be with her and we love you."

Chapter 15
DARLENE SEAY

Darlene and I met when I first started taking hand-dance lessons with the Charm City Hand-Dancers under the instructions of Shirley Duncan and her team of instructors: Reggie, Tina, Lewis, and Wayne. For those not familiar with hand-dancing, I would compare it to old-fashioned swing dancing or jive. Partners almost always hold hands, thus the name. As the years continued with our relationship in hand-dancing, so did our relationship with one another to the extent that we became very good friends. I so adore her daughter, Shervee, and Craig did as well. Darlene and Craig hit it off instantly, mainly because she was a perfect audience for listening to his great tales. When she learned of his home improvement business, she hired him to do work for her at the "friends' discount. I chuckled at how he used to give her an earful of his workday when he did work for her at the end of his workday. But, she seemed to never mind. They also had their own personal "jokes" from this relationship, that of course cannot be shared!

I can't remember when I actually told Darlene of Craig's illness. She was one of the few persons that I shared information with regarding my own personal health challenge at the time. Darlene is one of those friends that you know can keep your secrets. She is also one that will do whatever it is she can, if she really regards you as a friend. During the time of the back and forth treatments of Craig's, we would meet at our usual spot. It was my time to vent. And she had no problem asking the questions. It really helped. But our meeting-up was not all doom and gloom; there were times of laughter, about anything, oftentimes with tears rolling down our eyes. During those times, we both needed to share our challenges.

When Darlene reached out to me to say that she wanted to make a trip to come out to our home in West Virginia along with Emanuel, Craig and I were happy to receive her and Emanuel. True, this was not her first visit. We had some great times with the whole gang: Happy, Tina, Pam, Annie, and others, whenever we went down for our so-called girlfriend weekend. But this time, it was a visit that she knew would be one that meant it would be the last time for her friend, her buddy. She too got the call from me when I learned the medical team at the Cancer Treatment Center had advised him that his prognosis was poor and they had no other treatment alternatives. Still she came. Darlene shared the following...

Q: What would you say about the title of the book in regards to Craig?

A: The title is very appropriate and sounds like Craig embracing his sense of humor even until the very end. He always had a wonderful sense of humor, and that is the one thing I miss most about him.

Q: Can you remember the first conversation you had with Craig about his diagnosis?

A: We never really discussed his illness or his diagnosis. He would always share his own little private jokes or anecdotes with me like, "You know I got a man for that!" (Smile)

Q: How often were you able to spend time with him during his illness?

A: I got to spend time with Craig a few times between his treatments at Johns Hopkins and Philadelphia at different times, and I hold onto and cherish those memories dearly.

Q: What is your fondest memory of Craig?

A: Emanuel and I visited Craig at his home two weeks prior to his passing. We drove two hours through a rainstorm and just when we arrived at his home in West Virginia, the rain completely stopped. It was as though angels were smiling down upon us. Cookie took us around and showed us the facilities (spa, tennis court, golf course, rec room, etc.). While we were gone, he baked a homemade strawberry shortcake for us. I couldn't believe it. Who does something like that as sick as he was? Craig did. Only he would do something like that.

Q: How was your life changed or been impacted by Craig in his final days?

A: Craig taught me how to live with courage, character, and conviction, and he showed me what true love means. If I don't meet another person like him on this earth again (and I don't expect to) I know I have been truly blessed by knowing him.

Q: If you could say or share something with him today, what would that be?

A: I would tell him," Thank you. Thank you for showing me grace, the character and the quality of a man that you are, and you will always be in my heart. You lived your life to the fullest and did not waste one second of it. You did not merely exist, you lived your life without one second of regret. Craig, you lived, loved and shared life for us all to see." He accepted his place and his time on Earth with us, and when he was through, he extended his hand to God and walked gracefully and courageously with him to the other side.

Chapter 16
HAPPY MITCHELL AND CLAUDE DODSON

Happy and Claude often visited us in our home in West Virginia. Happy was also met when I began to learn how to hand-dance. She also was part of the tenth graduating class of the Charm City Hand-Dancers. Happy and I hit it off instantly, and we claimed each other as sisters. Since the time of our meeting, we have remained dear friends to one another. When we did the "girlfriend" thing in West Virginia, Happy was indoctrinated into the fold. Happy has always had an intriguing way about her, often not really understood by others. She has a style of dancing that is unique. Darlene and I would often imitate it, the way she had her hands flailing out, and eyelashes batting as she would look into the eyes of her dance partners. I would often say, "To know Happy is to love Happy," and nothing else could be said. At our tenth class graduation, Happy decided that she would do a performance to honor Shirley, the President of the Charm City Hand-Dancers. It never mattered to Happy that she did not get the approval, she just wanted to do her performance; that was our Happy. It nearly destroyed everything we all worked so hard to accomplish that day. But because we were family, we never held that against Happy, and she still remains a part of this family until this day.

Claude joined the groups of visitors to our home when he and Happy became an item. Since he was Happy's significant other, it was only natural that he would be received and accepted by Craig and me with open arms. I always liked Claude, as he was very direct and knowledgeable about a lot of things, and in my opinion, one of the best hand-dancers I ever encountered.

He and Craig hit it off instantly. Claude was often so amused by Craig's worldly tales. I wished Craig had the rhythm of Claude, but it seemed that he possessed the "white-boys" moves and Claude had the "black-guy" moves. The only dance Craig really got down was the Electric Slide, and he was always a half-note off in that dance. When we were moving down and on the way up in the dance, Craig would just be moving down and be a half-move up when we would be on our way moving back, and then get angry if someone stepped on his toes when he was too slow in his moves. When Claude learned of Craig's illness, he and Happy would call from time-to-time to see how he was coming along.

I am told that when the news of Craig's time coming close to an end, it was Claude who prompted Happy to call me to schedule a visit to come up to West Virginia to see us. Claude was very insistent that they make that visit right away. I felt that he really needed for Craig to know that he had not forgotten him; and wanted to let him know that he was there to do whatever he could for him. Craig was on hospice then and remained home. When Happy called, she said she and Claude wanted to come and right away. They came to see us on a rainy Friday in August.

Happy wanted the occasion to be a "happy" one. She came with party hats and sparkly table settings to show Craig that their visit would be bright and fun-filled. The decision to go out to get Chinese food was one that I am sure Claude will never forget. This was another of Craig's food cravings. The rain did not seem to be letting up, so rather than us all leave out together for a bite, Craig and Claude decided to ride together to the Chinese restaurant, with Claude driving and Craig navigating. I don't think Claude realized what he was embarking upon as Craig navigated him through the so-called short-cut route. Claude told me when he got back that it was one of the most intense drives he had ever taken. His eyes were still bugged out when they returned.

When they got back, Happy and I had consumed a couple of glasses of wine. She made the table very pretty with the sparkles and party hats, and matching knives, forks, and paper plates. We all ate, drank, caught up on all the gossip of the hand-dance community, and watched a couple of movies together. I think we all knew that this would be their last time seeing Craig, but I also knew that in their hearts they felt a sense of closure because they were there to lift up his spirits so he would not have to think about himself for a while. This too, was one other wonderful time that I was able to share with my closest friends and Craig. Here are the words that Happy shared about Craig.

Q: What would you say about the title of the book in regards to Craig?

A: Wow, the title of the book sounds just like him. That's Craig. It speaks to his acceptance of the situation.

Q: Can you remember the first conversation you had with Craig or Cookie about his diagnosis? What was your response and reaction to the news?

A: When I first heard about his diagnosis, I was devastated. Craig was so full of life. He enjoyed life and wanted to embrace it and he shared his life with everyone that he met. I really loved Craig. He would sit down and share his experiences and explain things to you.

Q: How often did you meet with him during this time?

A: During his illness, I met with him three or four times, but they were beautiful times. He did not make it sad. He was still responsive and talking just like old Craig. He treated me special. I know I was Cookie's friend, but he always treated me so special. It's funny how when you haven't thought about someone for a long time and you realize how much you really, really, miss them. You still have a hole in your heart from them.

Q: How was your life impacted or changed while visiting or talking with him in his final days?

A: I know that if I ever get in that situation like him, I know I would have to be like him and share it with other people to embrace it and not be afraid. I know that I would have to be able to accept it and not to be afraid so that hopefully somebody else can learn from me.

Q: What is your fondest memory of Craig?

A: My fondest memory of Craig is of him taking me out in the canoe on the lake at his home in West Virginia. He knew I was afraid of the water and could not swim. He helped me conquer a fear that day of being on the water and not being able to swim and I thank him for that.

Q: If you could share or say anything to him today, what would that be?

A: "Craig, I am so glad that I met you. I loved you for being yourself and for the way you treated and respected your wife, Cookie, and how you treated her friends like they were your friends, like they were family. And, I want to say thank you, Craig, and you will always have a place in my heart. I love you, Craig!

Chapter 17
EMANUEL BROWN

Emanuel too was someone that I met in my hand-dance world. In fact, he ended up as my dance partner at the tenth Charm City graduating hand-dance class. During that time, we often practiced for the graduation, under the tutelage of our no-nonsense but great instructor, Reggie Goodman. I still laugh when I think of one particular turn that Emanuel would always fall through during the times we practiced, but we got through our routine and had a great time at our graduation. I know we all miss those times. Emanuel was always laughing and had such a good spirit. We of the tenth graduating class still support each other from time to time, when we feel the need.

The call from Darlene was no surprise, but when Emanuel called me after learning of Craig's illness, I was somewhat surprised, but very happy to hear from him. Our tenth graduating class was like family; I should have remembered that. I also knew that Emanuel could identify with what I was going through, having walked that walk in his life, he could relate. So when he called to come down and visit with us, we were happy to receive him. It was another very rainy day as I remember. The average person would have been intimidated driving through those mountains, but not Emanuel; of course he had his sidekick Darlene egging him on with, "You can do it."

Emanuel was amused by what he saw during his visit. The evening of Darlene and Emanuel's visit, Craig had a desire for a strawberry shortcake. He had developed several food cravings during this time, that were always satisfied by visits from family and friends. I was glad that he wanted to eat. This time, he wanted to make the cake himself. When Darlene and Emanuel visited, he was in the beginning stages.

Our afternoon together started with regular conversations. I noticed Craig and Emanuel enjoying their own private conversation while Darlene and I continued our conversation about various subjects. It was a fun-filled and humorous visit. I took them both on a tour of the area, in the hopes that the cake would be ready on our return. When we got back, the cake was ready, and cooling down for the cool-whip icing. We continued with the meal that was prepared for them, drank much wine, and finished the evening with the best strawberry shortcake we have ever eaten! It was such a great time shared with Darlene and Emanuel and I will be forever indebted to them for taking the time to be with Craig in his final days. Emanuel expressed the following...

Q: What would you say about the title of the book as it relates to Craig?

A: I think the title is pretty catchy. I think this title summarizes Craig's struggle with his demon (cancer) before his death. I believe the title in and of itself conveys to others struggling with or going through a life-changing event that it's all right to come to terms with an issue and to continue with life with as much vigor as one can muster. It says that each and every one will ultimately go through a life or death struggle and not everyone is given the chance to grow old; so appreciate, use wisely, and give thanks for every single day of your life.

Q: Can you remember the first conversation you had with Craig about his diagnosis?

A: When I heard of Craig's illness, myself and one other friend (Darlene) visited with him at his home in Hedgesville, West Virginia. Craig was open, warm, and forthcoming with his comments concerning his diagnosis and the final outcome as articulated by his physician to him. I met Craig several months after his diagnosis and by that time, Craig had totally accepted his fate. He, however, was upbeat and positive. In fact, he went into the kitchen and in his positive can-do attitude proceeded to bake a strawberry shortcake that the entire party enjoyed. We drank strawberry sangria and enjoyed the time we had.

Q: What was your response and reaction to the news?

A: When I heard of Craig's illness, I was in awe, shock, disillusioned, thwarted, and in sheer disbelief. How could this happen to Craig, a man full of life, a man with a future, a man that planned to work, a man that worked his plan?

Q: How often did you meet with him during this time?

A: I only met Craig twice before his death, but the final occasion that we met demonstrated his enthusiasm and attitude toward both life and death. He shared with me in a very humbling and unselfish way that not everything in life is meant to last forever, so learn to let go and move on. I felt that he had come to terms with his illness and he knew that shortly his time in this life would end.

Q: How was your life changed or impacted while visiting and talking with him in his final days?

A: I think that Craig's attitude and wherewithal to knowingly accept his final calling is an attribute that I myself hope that if given the opportunity can accept that change with the same level of dignity as he did.

Q: What is your fondest memory of Craig?

:A Several months before Craig's passing, he and his wife Cookie attended my retirement party at Ft. Meade, Maryland and I must say that never once during this affair did he acknowledge or ever give any indication that he was in a bout for his life. Never once did his expression or emotions show anything but homage for my situation. He was Craig, a smooth and debonair gentleman until the end.

Q: If you could say or share anything with him today, what would that be?

A: "Brother, you've done well, you fought a good fight."

Chapter 18
REVEREND PENELOPE GLADWELL

The adage that people are in your life for a reason, a season, or a lifetime is so befitting for my new friend, Rev. Gladwell. She truly was there for me in this season, and I can say with true conviction, she will be a part of my life until the end. Especially now as my Facebook friend!

Time was getting close to the end for Craig. I knew it was time to put plans in place for his arrangements. I wanted so badly to have someone from the clergy come and pray with him. We were members of a church in Baltimore. Craig rarely attended, but I continued to attend whenever I could when in Baltimore, and we both remained on the roster. My church did, however, add him to their prayer list. I wasn't sure if such a drive would be amenable to my pastor, but I really felt a need to have someone come to pray with him. One afternoon I happened to see Craig sitting on the couch with his eyes closed, and his lips were moving at the time. I asked him, "Are you okay? What are you doing?"

He replied, "Talking to God." I left the room so he could have his time.

That Monday, I placed a call to Hedgesville Chapel and when explaining my purpose of the call, was given the number of Rev. Blackwell to call to get information about having a service at the chapel. I knew that Craig's final wishes were to have his ashes spread in the lake behind us. I had attended the chapel a few times since we'd moved to West Virginia; the parishioners were always so friendly and warm. I then called this second number, and again explained the purpose of my call and inquired about having a service at the chapel and using the hall adjacent to the chapel. I expressed that I didn't expect my husband to go the next day or so, but that I felt it was time to begin the planning. The woman I spoke to was Rev. Penny Gladwell. She provided me with information on whom to contact about using the hall; she also offered to come by and visit with Craig at our home. I was touched by her kindness and benevolence.

A few weeks later, Craig was in the hospital the last time. I wasn't sure if he would make it through that weekend. I told Craig that I had spoken to a kind person, who was a minister, and she offered to come out and have prayer with him. He agreed. Rev. Blackwell shared the following:

"As I walked down the hallway of the hospital, I had no idea what I would find. Several weeks before, a woman had called my home, introducing herself and asking for funeral information. Her husband was dying, she told me, and since he loved it here in West Virginia, she wanted the services to be here.

"I asked to come by and visit with him at home, but the opportunity never presented itself. Now Craig was hospitalized and would be kept comfortable there until he died. I wanted to meet with him if I could.

"As I pushed open the door to his room I was greeted warmly by Cookie and the other close friends gathered around Craig's bed. He seemed to be dozing, but stirred and opened his eyes when he heard voices. I introduced myself and told him I had been waiting to meet him. He smiled just a little. Then he asked the nurse to help him sit up a bit. He swung his legs over the side of the bed and sat up, struggling with each breath, and yet seeming to want to be able to have a conversation with me.

"I told him I wanted to reassure him that he was deeply loved by God, and that Jesus was in the room, ready to help him through the process of entering life eternal. He looked at me and said 'thank you' in a weak whisper.

When I asked him if I could pray with him, he nodded. The others in the room joined us. Standing in that small circle, we thanked God for Craig's life. We asked God to be especially close and real to us. We asked for the Holy Spirit to fill the room and make it a holy place for these final days of Craig's earthly life.

"When the prayer ended, we were all teary. Craig took both my hands and whispered 'thank you' again. Then he slumped back into the bed and settled against the pillow. Was it my imagination that his face was more peaceful? That his presence was less agitated?

"I hugged each of the friends in the room and bid my goodbyes. That was Saturday, September 11, 2012. Craig passed that Sunday, September 12."

Chapter 19
OTHER FRIENDS

Smitty

There were other friends who were so wonderful and so important to us during this journey. Smitty was one of those friends. I and Pam reached out to him several times for this endeavor. I have concluded that revisiting this journey with Smitty was too difficult for him. But, I know I would be remiss and I know in my heart Craig would want me to share just how phenomenal Smitty was during this time.

I think Smitty and his significant other, Tina, visited us more than anyone else in our home in West Virginia. When we made the permanent move, Craig would often wait for me over at Smitty's until I finished my classes at Coppin State University. Sometimes we stayed overnight with them. The two of them loved to cook. Smitty and Craig were brothers at heart. They shared a love of cooking and would make the best dishes at the July 4th cookouts at Smitty's home in Baltimore, or our home in West Virginia. As I understand it, their acquaintance with one another started at a local bar in the neighborhood where Smitty resided. Craig often stopped off there on his way home when we lived in Baltimore City and then Owings Mills, Maryland. Their relationship continued even when there were, from time to time, some contentious happenings at this local spot.

I did visit with Craig at his neighborhood spot on some occasions and even though I felt it was not a place of my social world, I always ended up enjoying myself and enjoyed meeting his friends. It was there that I met Tina and we "hit it off" well. So whenever they visited with us, we would enjoy our "girl talk" together while the two of them attended to the grill or be out back fishing. On one particular occasion, Smitty fell out of the canoe while they were fishing, even after Craig had warned him that standing up would cause the canoe to tip over. If Smitty had to share a memory of Craig's, I think this would be one of his best memories. He was a soggy mess when he came inside, and I surely did not appreciate how muddy he was. But it ended up being a laughing occasion, as many of them were.

The news of Craig's illness was traumatic to Tina and Smitty both, but especially for Smitty. Smitty had worked with Craig during the times he was employed by Ray. Craig had Smitty work with him so that he could get back on his feet as he was going through some difficult times. During the earlier months of Craig's illness, he would go to Smitty's home and visit with him after his treatments. As time continued on, and Craig was at a point where he was not doing much at the job sites anymore, Craig would drive into town with me and stay with Smitty all day until I got off from work. I think one of the fondest memories of Craig and Tina was the time Craig went on his last trip with them to do some crabbing. They all loved to eat crabs and equally loved catching and cooking them. They made a trip to the bay that day and had big plans to bring home a lot of crabs. I really can't remember how successful they were that day with their catch, I just remembered how wiped out Craig was on his return. I think this week was a week of "final loves" for Craig's hobbies. This too was the week of his last plane flight with his friend Stan. He seemed to really get quite weak after those two outings.

The call to Tina and Smitty was a call with much weeping. When Smitty came to view Craig's body in Baltimore, he completely lost control. The day of the funeral in West Virginia, Smitty could not make it. Tina said it was just too much for him. I spoke to Smitty a few times after Craig's passing. We promised to get together and have him get back out there on the grill. Perhaps we will. To Smitty and Tina, please know that you will never be forgotten for all of your and support in our times of need. Thank you so much for being such great friends.

Paul and Dot Beckham

I met Paul and Dot during my first years dating Craig. Paul was another one of Craig's closest and best friends. I know that Paul was on the list of top ten folk that Craig called when he learned of his diagnosis. I believed that friendship was one of the longest of all of his friends. Craig loved Paul's wife, Doretha, and she too held Craig in such a high regard. When Pam reached out to Paul for the book, it was obvious to me that while his intentions were good to respond, there were other important issues going on in his life. I know Paul and Dot will never forget Craig and I know they still think of him until this day.

Outside of Drake, Craig's brother, Paul would be the next person most visited by Craig. They had a common interest in eating well and drinking often. But Paul was not a drinker of cheap beer, he was a connoisseur of fine foods and only the top shelf alcoholic beverages. Paul and Craig made some great dishes during those times. I can remember Craig coming home late at night after they made some great meals together. Craig was at Paul and Dot's wedding, he was there through the births of their daughters, and there for many celebrations throughout our twenty-one years of marriage.

Both Paul and Dot visited us in West Virginia during his final days. That too was a great and joyful visit. Both Dot and I had been going through our own health challenges; however, we still were able to help Craig take his mind off of himself for a while. I know they would have had many great memories to share and I know that his impact on their lives could only be told by them. What I do remember is that on the weekend before Craig passed away, Paul and Dot were away on vacation. It seemed that Craig knew that it would be his last weekend. He started calling out the names of some of his friends, and Paul was one of them. I heard him yell out "Paul," and when that happened, I went to his side and said, "Honey, Paul is away on vacation, remember?" He said "Paul" again. I explained again that Paul was away on vacation; however, I assured him that I would leave a voice message on Paul's phone to let him know that he was in the hospital. He seemed fine with that answer.

Paul and Dot never made it to the hospital. I am not sure how they even got the news of Craig's passing, but they cut their vacation short and attended the services in West Virginia. That was the kind of friends Paul and Dot were to Craig. I know Craig would want them both spoken of as I write about his journey with lung cancer. I too want them to know that I will never forget the many wonderful times we shared with one another and I will forever keep them in my thoughts and prayers.

Chapter 20
THE FINAL THIRTY DAYS

When Craig and I packed his things up from the hospital, we were advised to call a hospice team once we got back to West Virginia. But first things first: we went on our cruise. I was able to convince the physician, one of whom we had never met, to write a prescription for prednisone with all of the other prescriptions that he needed. I knew that his appetite would be increased with that medication, and even though his oncologist was not in total agreement, it was too late by then. The plan was in place so that he could eat on the cruise and enjoy himself, and eat he did!

The ship sailed from Baltimore to Bermuda, then New England, and then back to Baltimore. On this second cruise, my granddaughter Quierra, my friend Pinky, and her children Reena and Amar went. Craig was very comfortable with having his personal nurse Pinky on the cruise. Overall, he did quite well. He drank his beer and ate often times two meals at one sitting. I was taught that one is never to leave a dinner table until all have finished their meals. We knew that this was to be proper etiquette; however, when a second or third meal is asked for, etiquette can go out the window, or in this case, overboard. By day three, we were getting tired of waiting for him to finish all of his meals, and he didn't mind that the young people left. It was just Pinky and myself that had to wait until all was consumed properly.

We continued the cruise and attempted a couple of excursions (tours) of New England, leaving the ship. There was only one time when we had to end one of the tours early because Craig started to feel a little ill. When we got back to the ship, his meds were administered. By then, his pain meds were being administered around the clock. There could be no deviations. On this occasion, Craig's previous meal had been removed from the room by the housekeeping staff, and he raised some holy hell because of it. I had to call the kitchen so that they could bring another tray of food. They apologized for the inconvenience; they assumed that the tray of food was to be discarded. One would have thought that this was going to be Craig's only meal. He remained cantankerous until the end.

We thankfully got back home safely from the cruise. When we got back home, we started our plans for hospice care. We were able to have one of the physicians working at the local hospital be his primary care and consulting physician until the end. The hospice team referred to this transition of life as 'living your life until the end' as opposed to dying until the end. We were not expected to stay home. They stated we could go anywhere we wanted. We just needed to let the hospice team know. We accepted that philosophy and that's what we did. Craig and I often took walks around our lake, and we talked about what his wishes were for the end of his life. That was hard for me, but he did that very gently.

Craig knew how much enjoyment I got from dancing; he knew that my life prior to it was filled with the care management and caregiving of my mother, father, and sister. He knew I needed an outlet, so he never complained when I wanted to do something related to the dance world. I chuckled when he mentioned in one of our walks how he would consider taking lessons so he could go dancing with me.

During this time, we also knew it was time to meet with our attorney to discuss how to manage our debts with only one income. I was wise enough to have obtained cancer insurance for us both, which helped a lot. We were able to get resolution for our debts; Craig hung in there for me so I would not have to get through this financial quagmire alone. Our conversations about finances earlier in our marriage did not end well. Toward the end, however, we were in accord.

The hospice team visited us often from late July to September. During that time, Craig had two hospitalizations. During the first hospitalization, his family and I thought it was the end. So many drove up to see him in West Virginia. But he stabilized to the extent where he could be discharged. I can remember the surprise of family and friends when they came to visit him. To their surprise, they found him looking good and he was soon discharged to return home.

When Craig got back home, he still continued to take the drive to and from West Virginia to stay with Smitty for a while. After his last crabbing trip. He felt that he no longer could make the drive. Family and friends continued to visit with us. We set up our home in West Virginia for the hospice visits. I hired an outside agency to sit with him and to make sure that he would eat while I was at work in between the times when hospice could not be there. I also needed to have someone there when I was out on an appointment. I understand that there are several stages to the dying process, depending on whose information you are referencing. I think the decision is unanimous with the final stage being acceptance. Craig had accepted his fate; however, he still wanted to be as free of pain as possible, and he still wanted to be as comfortable as possible. Because his breathing had become more difficult, he was put on oxygen as he needed. Even then he never lost his cantankerousness. Once when the company delivered the tanks and advised him of the settings, Craig felt that the air flow was not working properly. He immediately got back on the phone and had the company come back, reset the settings, and bring all new tanks!

Craig also never wanted to waiver from his 'husbandly duties' when it came to the bedroom, even during that time. He kept his noisy oxygen concentrator in the bedroom and kept his portable close by in the event he needed more air during our times of intimacy. I wanted more often than not to say, "Moozie, how about not worrying about me right about now, just save all of your air for yourself." I just did not have the nerve.

I knew it was time to make arrangements as July went into August and August went into September. It was way past the three weeks or less as diagnosed by the physicians at the Cancer Treatment Center. I had begun to believe he was going to have at least six more months, and that maybe he would even make it through the Thanksgiving and Christmas holidays. I decided to start making the arrangements with the Hedgesville Chapel and March's funeral home, however. My sister Sissy Gloria went with me during that time. I needed support; she and I had buried our brother Mike a year before, so she was able to help me maneuver through this process. My hopes were soon diminished after a phone call on September 10th, 2012 that changed everything.

I received a call from Sherrie as I was leaving work that day. I had completed the paperwork for FMLA (Family Medical Leave Act), and felt that the time had come to be at home with my husband around the clock. I had a social worker on vacation the following week and had planned that on her return, my leave would start.

Sherrie said to me that Craig kept telling her to call 911. I asked Sherrie why he was doing that, and she stated she was not sure, "He just keeps saying 'call 911'." Sherrie had decided to come over and stay with Craig until I got home that evening. The fact that Craig was giving his friend such as hard time seemed very strange to me. I asked Sherrie to put Craig on the phone, and I asked him what was wrong.

He said, "Tell her to call 911." He never explained why he wanted 911, I knew hospice was still following his care, and I asked Craig to let Sherrie call the hospice team for him. He did not want the hospice team, and he insisted on her calling 911.

I said to Sherrie, "Please just do what he asks. I am on my way home." I drove the hour and a half to West Virginia, exceeding all of the speed limits. I prayed all the way home to God to please don't let him die until I get there to City Hospital in West Virginia. I could hardly see as the tears were flowing down my cheeks. I was so lost and so afraid.

When I got to the hospital, Craig had only been there a few minutes. Sherrie met me in the emergency room. I announced myself and flew back to the room with Craig. This was a scene that I had experienced too often. Craig seemed stable enough; he never lost consciousness. By then his blood pressure had dropped very low. I had to answer what I thought to be the same questions that I had answered what seemed to be a hundred times. I had become so disgusted with the whole healthcare arena. I was not at all pleased with the way things were going with the hospice team either. When his doctor came in, he told me that the cancer was now in all of Craig's major organs. His physician stated that he knew by now I was very weary, and if I wanted him to remain at the hospital to continue Craig's care, he would. He said Craig would probably not last the weekend. I said, "Absolutely not, I want Craig to pass away at home."

Craig looked up at the doctor and said, softly, "No, I don't want her to go through anymore. I want to stay here."

I then cried-out, "No way, he's coming home!"

His physician looked at us both and realized we needed time to talk, to come to some conclusion, and he left us to discuss what the next course of action would be. I then started pleading with Craig. I said, "Please, you need to be at home."

But he said, "I've put you through enough. I can't put you through anymore."

I shook my head and told Craig that I was going to call Drake, his brother, so that he could convince him to come home with me and die at home. I telephoned Drake and told him what had occurred and how we'd ended up at the hospital. I also asked Drake to help me convince Craig to come at home to die. Craig and Drake talked for a little while and after their conversation, I knew that Craig was going to have his way. He wanted to remain at the hospital in his final days. I first thought that he was just not satisfied with the hospice team, and that he did not trust them enough to manage his care. But when he said to me, "I can't have you waking up every day with memories of me dying at home, on the sofa." I realized that there was nothing else to discuss. His mind was made up. As usual, he was putting me first, before his own needs. That was Craig.

The final calls were made to family and friends yet again. Certain names were called at the end and they were the ones that I called, and most of them did show up. During that weekend, from Friday to that Sunday, they came; friends and family alike. Craig kept taking the oxygen tube out of his nose. He did not seem to want it anymore. I will never understand how he knew that that weekend would be the weekend of his passing. The day I saw his eyes closed and he told me that he as praying perhaps was when it was revealed to him that it would be the weekend. The visit from Rev. Penny Gladwell that Saturday I think helped this transition. I knew how important it was to have his final goodbyes with his Godson and nephew, Chris. I have been told that when one is transitioning, hearing is one of the last senses to go. So in a soft voice that Sunday morning, I whispered to him that Chris was on his way. I believe he heard me when I said that because he passed as soon as Chris arrived and bid him goodbye. My dearest husband of twenty-one years passed on September 12, 2012 after his battle with lung cancer.

Marriage and child-rearing are two of the most difficult life experiences ever endeavored by anyone. It is never what we hope and dream of. We want them both to be pleasant and nearly perfect, without too much drama. But it is never that way. Craig's and my marriage was not without its problems either. His vitriolic remarks were sometimes too much for me. We had periods when I felt we were married in name only, and our behaviors reflected so. Oftentimes the examples we grow up with greatly influence what we think a marriage should or should not be about. I was influenced by a mother who remained married to a man for over fifty years, doing everything for him and her children, all the while having little or nothing of herself to rely on. My dad was a strong and dominating man, never conceding to anyone or anything. At different times, I became both of them during our marriage. I accepted things that I probably shouldn't have, and often struck back in ways that I shouldn't have to keep my own sense of self. Craig too, spoke of how he was so hurt and torn by the breakup of his parents' marriage. His mom was the most sensitive and fun-loving person I knew, and his dad a no nonsense disciplinarian, with a tongue that could cut you to the core. Craig was the embodiment of both.

But for whatever reason, we chose to stay with one another and continue to figure out how to make things work. It did not take me long to realize that a good man is hard to find. Craig helped me to realize that and I will never, ever have any regrets about staying married to him for so long. Craig loved flying. He used to say in his terms of flying, that one should never leave his wing man. When he became ill, I knew that I was his "wing man." He never had to worry about me not being there for him. I was there every step of the way. I truly did not want his life to end the way it did. We had plans to live the rest of our days in the mountains of West Virginia. If he had to die young, I wanted him to die doing one of his great adventures. Perhaps, had that happened, this book would not have been written.

But I knew he would come. I just did not expect him to come so soon after passing away. My mommy came to me after she passed away in 1995. Craig was there with me in bed the night she came to visit me. Everyone had returned to their homes by then. My wonderful friends (Val, Pam, and Annie) had returned home to their lives after staying over with me before and after the funeral. My son and my grands had returned to their homes after spending a week with me. I knew I needed another week of reprieve, so that Sunday, a week after everyone had left, he came, just like my mommy did; Craig came. He came quietly in the night, as I lay asleep. I felt the bed go down, and he assumed his spoon position; that's how we often slept together at night, except when he would sleep in our Jacuzzi tub, very often. I'm not sure as to how I managed to see his face, but I did. He had a look of concern for me, and as I cried he whispered to me, "It's okay." I also remember him saying, "It was time," and he put his fingers to his mouth to shush my crying. The next thing I remember was that I woke up later in the morning, looking for Craig, only to remember that my life had changed and would never be the same. I was completely on my own after twenty-one years of marriage. But his visit confirmed that he would be with me in death as he was in life. And, I am fine with that!

I have moved on with my life since Craig's passing in 2012. It has been my faith and sense of self, along with a great network of friends and family, that has gotten me through it all. I know so many people have had to walk this journey, and I hope they too have received some comfort in the conversations shared by those who knew Craig and as they reflect upon their own loved one's journey. I did not want to write this book, but am happy that I have, because through writing it, closure has not only come to me, but to those who took this journey with him. I don't hear much from his friends anymore, so it was great that they responded to our requests for an interview. I do know that if it were the other way around, meaning if one of his dearest friends' significant other or spouse had passed away, he would be there constantly to make sure they were doing okay. That's just how he was. I am in touch constantly with his family, however. That's the convenience of Facebook! As I continue to live, I know that I will continue to write. I pray that future writing will be a less difficult endeavor.

Chapter 21
PAMELA PITT'S TRIBUTE

As stated in the introduction, this endeavor would not have taken place had it not been for the efforts of my dear friend Pam. I believe this task was as difficult for me as it was for her. Often times in penning the interviews for the final manuscript, I would have to stop and have my cries for so many of the memories shared and expressed by family and friends. But I realized that Pam also had to stop and shed her tears as she gathered up the conversations shared by so many. She has brought her closure through penning the final chapter. She summarizes this experience with the following words that she has entitled: Craig's Tribute. Here it is.

Dear Craig D. Sanders,

Thank you for coming into our lives and leaving an indelible fingerprint stamped on our hearts. You taught each and every one of us something about courage, strength, and wisdom in the way you lived your life, as well as how gracefully you surrendered your life to God.

Drake fondly remembers your devotion, dedication, and the caring that you always showed to those you loved, only as a brother can. You challenged and encouraged him to try new things such as skiing and scuba diving. It's not easy to say "goodbye" to your best friend in the world, so for now, he'll just say, "So long, see you again."

To your dear friend and buddy Ray, you were his little "MacGyver." Every place he goes in his home, there is a piece if you. Just as Jesus was known as the master carpenter, you were the master builder, who could build or fix anything. The Lord blesses us with many gifts and talents that you offered so generously to the world. You were an avid pilot and you soared above God's creations. You were an outstanding mechanic who could keep anything running and of course like Noah the builder, a creator of many things.

Stepmom Augustine's fondest memories are of family cookouts partaking of the Master Chef's barbeque skills. Everybody knows how you loved to cook and eat, the stranger the food the better, from pig's tail, squirrel, rabbit, and turtle, to those nasty chitterlings. "Yuk!"

Generosity of heart and showing others the meaning of true love is the gift that all of us who visited you at the cabin will be forever shared. How many times did you and Cookie fling open your doors for me, Darlene, Happy, Pinky, Annie, Val, Tina, and the many hosts of other guests that you welcomed with your hospitality, good food, crazy sense of humor and of course, "Getting our drink on!"

In your weakest moments, you did not hesitate to give your heart even when it was in a weakened state. Pinky said it best: "That's the sign of unconditional love." You lived your life to the fullest, and you did it your way. And in doing so, you left us with a valuable lesson. You showed us how to love one another, to face our fears, and to be grateful for the life that we have.

Craig, you understood that love is everlasting. We can never be separated from it. Because God is love and our love for you is eternal.

Cookie, I thank you for the honor and privilege of allowing me to capture the essence and the beauty of such a wonderful man, friend, and husband. There is not a day that goes by that I don't think about or miss my beloved Craig. I remember your wedding day like it was yesterday and I am so humbled and blessed to have been able to share many days and fun times with the two of you since then. You were blessed with twenty-one years together here on Earth and now you await time and eternity together.

LOVE ALWAYS, PAM

Review Requested:
If you loved this book, would you please provide a review at Amazon.com?

CPSIA information can be obtained
at www.ICGtesting.com
Printed in the USA
LVOW12s1055270916

506385LV00001B/25/P

9 781681 817903